READING

At the Middle and High School Levels:

Building Active Readers Across the Curriculum

✳

Second Edition

EDUCATIONAL RESEARCH SERVICE

2000 Clarendon Boulevard • Arlington, Virginia • 22201-2908
General Phone: (703) 243-2100 • Fax: (703) 243-5971
Publication Orders Phone: (800) 791-9308 • Fax: (800) 791-9309
Web site: www.ers.org • E-mail: ers@ers.org

The Information Source for School Decisions

Sponsored by:

American Association of School Administrators
American Association of School Personnel Administrators
Association of School Business Officials International
Council of Chief State School Officers
National Association of Elementary School Principals
National Association of Secondary School Principals
National School Public Relations Association

ERS President:
John M. Forsyth, Ph.D.

Educational Research Service is the nonprofit research foundation serving the research and information needs of education leaders and the public. ERS Comprehensive Subscriptions are available to local school districts, state and local associations of school administrators and school boards, state departments of education, and other related organizations.

Comprehensive subscription rates are graduated according to school district size or type of agency, and are available on request. For one annual fee, Comprehensive subscribers receive a broad range of resources, including:
- a copy of each new ERS report on priority concerns in education (12–15 per year);
- the monthly *ERS Bulletin,* summarizing research produced by other agencies;
- the quarterly *ERS Spectrum,* the journal of school research and information;
- the *ERS Informed Educator Series,* providing a comprehensive, yet concise eight-page overview of a priority topic in education each month;

- access for district administrators to ERS Custom Information Responses to meet their needs for information on specific topics and issues;
- access to the ERS Successful School Practices Collection, containing information about hundreds of successful programs in local school districts across the nation;
- *Successful School Practices,* published three times a year to summarize a sampling of programs and practices in the ERS Successful School Practices Collection;
- ERS School District Comparative Profiles, individually prepared reports on district revenues and expenditures, salaries and wages, and staffing ratios.

In addition to the ERS Comprehensive Subscription, educators can obtain Individual ERS Subscriptions bringing them the ERS resources of greatest interest to them. ERS reports are also available for purchase separately.

Publication Written by: Elizabeth A. Wilson
Research Support: Leila McLaurin Beasley, Research Specialist
Project Supervisor: Nancy J. Protheroe, Director, Special Research Projects

Ordering Information:

Stock No. 0340. Price of publication: For ERS Comprehensive subscribers: $9.00. For ERS Individual subscribers: $13.50. For Nonsubscribers: $18.00.

To order *Reading at the Middle and High School Levels: Building Active Readers Across the Curriculum, Second Edition,* contact ERS Member Services Information Center, 2000 Clarendon Boulevard, Arlington, VA 22201-2908. Phone: (800) 791-9308. Fax: (800) 791-9309. Web site: www.ers.org.

All mail orders must be accompanied by check, purchase order, or credit card information. Please add the greater of $3.50 or 10% of purchase price for postage and handling. Phone orders accepted with Visa, MasterCard, or American Express.

Table of Contents

FOREWORD V

SECTION ONE
INTRODUCTION: ISSUES SURROUNDING SECONDARY SCHOOL READING 1

Reading in the Content Areas 2
Older Students Lose Interest in Reading 4
Students At Risk of Reading Failure 6
Limited Time for Implementing Reading Strategies 7
Building Active Readers Across the Curriculum 7

SECTION TWO
MOTIVATIONAL FACTORS RELATED TO READING 9

Adolescent Developmental Needs 9
Internal Influences 10
  Attitude Toward Reading 11
  Interest in Reading 11
External Influences 12
  The Effects of Television 12
  Parent Involvement 13

SECTION THREE
APPROACHES FOR ACTIVELY ENGAGING STUDENTS IN READING 15

Encouraging Students to Read More and Read Widely 16
  Choice in Reading Materials 17
  Creating a Print-Rich Environment: Classroom and School Libraries 17
  Young Adult Literature in the Classroom 18
  Exposure to a Wide Variety of Materials 20
  In-School Free Reading 21
  Reading Aloud 22

Talking About Texts 24
  Small-Group Discussion 24
  Designing Small-Group Work 26
  Using Discussion Groups with At-Risk and Remedial Readers 27
  Cooperative Learning Groups in Content-Area Classrooms 28

Cultivating the Reading-Writing Connection 29
  Writing as a Pre-Reading Activity 30
  Dialogue Journals 30
  The Reading-Writing Connection in the Content Areas 32

Other Approaches 33
  Classroom Debate 33
  Thematic Units 34
  Reader's Theater 35
  Concept-Oriented Reading Instruction 35
  Computers and Reading Instruction 36

SECTION FOUR
METACOGNITION: DEVELOPING GOOD READING STRATEGIES 39

Pre-Reading Activities 41
Useful Strategies During Reading 42
  "Click or Clunk" Strategy 42

Reciprocal Teaching 43
SQ3R 44
Scan & Run 44
Directed Reading-Thinking Activity 45
Visual Representations 45
Embedded Questions 46
INSERT 47
Story Maps 47
Some Things to Keep in Mind When Teaching Metacognitive Strategies ... 47
Make Sure Learners Understand a Strategy's Purpose 48
Dismantle Ineffective Routines 48
Model the Use of a Strategy 48
Link Strategy Use to Learning Outcomes 49

SECTION FIVE
OTHER TECHNIQUES TO IMPROVE READING SKILLS 51
Vocabulary Development 51
Peer Tutoring 53
Some Guidelines for Establishing a Peer Tutoring Program 54

SECTION SIX
ASSESSMENT: PURPOSES AND APPROACHES 55
Approaches That Highlight Assessment as a Meaning-Making Process ... 56
Essays 57
Portfolios 58
Personal Anthologies 59
Other Alternative Evaluation Methods 59
Approaches Designed to Provide Teachers with Information on Student Reading Level 61
Teacher Observation 62
Cloze Procedure 62
Retellings 62
Miscue Analysis 63
Informal Reading Inventories (IRIs) 63

SECTION SEVEN
ISSUES SPECIFIC TO CONTENT-AREA READING INSTRUCTION 65
Reading Skills Needed in Some Specific Content Areas 65
Reading in Social Studies 66
Reading in Science 67
Reading in Mathematics 68
Using Literature in the Content-Area Classroom 69
Using Textbooks 70
Readability and Readability Formulas 71
Adapting Textbooks That Are in Use 72
Inservice on Using Textbooks Effectively 74

SECTION EIGHT
CONCLUSION 75

REFERENCES 77

Foreword

Educational Research Service is pleased to publish this second edition of *Reading at the Middle and High School Levels: Building Active Readers Across the Curriculum.* As with the first edition, published in 1995, the focus of the report is on strategies that educators can use to improve student reading skills and enhance interest in reading. Many of these strategies are applicable across the curriculum—not just in English classes, but also in subjects such as science and social studies. In addition, some suggestions are provided for using strategies in specific content area classrooms or with at-risk readers.

The introduction to this report asks: "Reading instruction—isn't that a topic for elementary education?" Yet those teachers and administrators who are working with middle and high school students know that reading-related issues continue to be important during a student's secondary school education, with new concerns added as students progress through the grades. Teachers ask: How can I interest the MTV generation in reading? What can I do if some of my students have difficulty reading the assigned text? With all the content that must be covered in the courses I teach, how can I effectively integrate reading instruction into my classes?

Reading at the Middle and High School Levels: Building Active Readers Across the Curriculum, Second Edition addresses these questions and more. This second edition incorporates relevant research since 1995, based on a thorough review of the literature conducted by the ERS research staff.

As with all the reports in the ERS "What We Know About" series, the context for the discussion is provided by research findings, informed opinions contained in the professional literature, and examples from school personnel of "what works." Topics addressed in this publication include: approaches for helping poor readers develop good reading strategies, ways to increase student interest in reading for pleasure, and ways that social studies, science, or math teachers might effectively incorporate reading instruction within their subject areas.

Reading at the Middle and High School Levels is written for practitioners—for teachers, school administrators, curriculum specialists, and staff development personnel—who understand reading as a key to success for their students, both during the school years and into adulthood. ERS hopes that this publication helps you nurture your students as active readers who are empowered to achieve their full academic potential.

John M. Forsyth, Ph. D.
President

Introduction:
Issues Surrounding Secondary School Reading

Reading instruction—isn't that a topic for elementary education? After all, most students at the middle and high school levels have already learned how to read.

Many people make this assumption about the relevance of reading to the secondary school curriculum. It may be true that most students master the basics of reading by the time they leave elementary school, but it is still important to consider some of the issues that make reading a critical concern at the middle and high school levels:

1) Reading in content areas such as science, mathematics, and social studies demands skills beyond those used in the early grades.

2) Students often lose interest in reading as they get older.

3) Large numbers of secondary students are at risk of reading failure, and they require reading instruction that is targeted to their needs.

4) Secondary teachers have limited time for implementing reading strategies, unless such strategies can be incorporated into approaches for teaching the curriculum.

❖ READING IN THE CONTENT AREAS ❖

By the time students reach middle school and high school, they are expected to have the comprehension skills necessary to read in the content areas. Reading in a content area poses new challenges to the secondary student; whereas elementary reading instruction focuses primarily on learning to read, secondary reading instruction focuses on *reading to learn*. That is, reading becomes a tool for gathering information about a subject area.

In addition, the reading material required of middle school and high school students becomes more difficult. Gone are the short stories filled with vivid characters and familiar topics that were the basis of the elementary reading program. At the secondary level, textbooks predominate—materials that often are compactly written and contain specialized vocabulary. Students must also learn to read the maps, graphs, charts, and tables that are scattered throughout their texts. Because of these demands on reading skills, secondary students with poor literacy skills are at risk in many of their subject-area courses. This may increase their chances of dropping out of school (Carbo 1994). In recent years, researchers have found that direct instruction in reading strategies contributes to student success. Such strategies will be described in Section Four.

One concern content-area teachers often express is how to increase student engagement with the subject. Often, students bring little interest to content classes and are simply there to fulfill basic course requirements. These students may have the skills necessary to read in the content areas, but their lack of interest reduces the amount they learn. The typical structure of a content-area class—centered around a compactly written textbook filled with concepts unfamiliar to the students—only serves to worsen the situation. In such cases, strategies are required that can engage students in their content-area reading materials.

Understandably, content-area teachers want to devote their instructional time to teaching the important concepts of their subject area. However, placing a high priority on this task may lead teachers to devalue the importance of teaching reading skills. One study found that content teachers emphasize the presentation of concepts and de-emphasize readiness activities such as presenting objectives and previewing concepts. In addition, many content teachers rely on the textbook instead of using a variety of instructional resources (Ratekin et al. 1985). Because some content-area teachers believe that all their students should read on grade level, they do not view reading instruction as their responsibility—despite the reality that not all students come to their classrooms with good reading skills.

Research findings suggest that these beliefs may pose a serious problem for content reading programs. A study of the factors that enhance or hinder content reading programs, conducted by surveying a random sampling of *Journal of Reading* (currently *Journal of Adolescent & Adult Literacy*) subscribers, found that the top hindrance—identified by 44 percent of respondents—was the belief that reading instruction is not the content teacher's responsibility (Gee and Forester 1988). Other factors identified as barriers to the content reading program (indicated by at least one-fourth of respondents) were lack of administrative support or leadership, lack of inservice education, the feeling on the part of content teachers that they are not qualified to guide students' reading, lack of personnel to coordinate programs, and the belief that such a program is not needed. Results from another study suggest an additional factor—most content-area teachers are not exposed to wide and diverse types of research about teaching reading in the content areas (Blanchard 1989).

Making time for content-area reading instruction is certainly not an easy task, especially given the time demands already placed on teachers. However, planning ahead to integrate such instruction into the curriculum can help to make content-area reading instruction possible, effective, and efficient, rather than just an add-on.

Yet, even when teachers find a strategy to be highly desirable, they might be concerned about the efficiency of introducing it in the classroom. Reading specialists can make an important difference in this case. These specialists should work in cooperation with the content teacher, optimally in the content-area classroom itself—where students are struggling with real reading tasks—rather than in separate lessons about reading (International Reading Association 1989). Because reading specialists understand the basic reading problems, they can suggest possible solutions to students or teachers, and can work directly with teachers to implement comprehension strategies. Content teachers will also need additional administrative support, especially in cases where reading specialists are not available. Administrative support means developing inservice programs, as well as providing teachers with planning time or time to meet with other teachers.

Evidence suggests that when teachers *do* create time for content-area reading instruction, it makes a difference. A study conducted by secondary school content-area teachers tested instructional strategies that might improve content-area reading (Santa 1988). Strategies that teachers found to be effective in improving content-area achievement included: activating background knowledge before reading by brainstorming about the meanings of key vocabulary terms; asking students to keep a journal of content-area concept definitions; and asking students to create their own learning guides, instead of relying on teacher-prepared materials.

Other tactics that may help include: teaching students reading strategies for coping with a textbook that is hard to understand; supplementing the textbook with a variety of other related materials (such as newspaper articles and videos); and including motivational class activities, such as cooperative learning groups and thematic units. Secondary students report a strong preference for engaging activities that supplement their textbooks—such as guest speakers, field trips, and cooperative learning groups. However, these instructional strategies are used infrequently (Schumm et al. 1992).

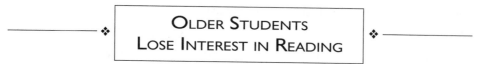

OLDER STUDENTS LOSE INTEREST IN READING

Sadly, at the same time that required reading skills become more challenging, the likelihood that students are reading for pleasure declines. This is an important point, since reading for fun has been linked to reading achievement. A government report based on the 1996 National Assessment of Educational Progress (NAEP) indicates that students who read daily for fun have higher average NAEP reading scores than students who never read for fun (National Center for Education Statistics 1997).

Although there are alternative explanations for this correlation—either that better readers enjoy reading and so read more, or that reading more actually contributes to reading competency—some combination of these two probably describes the relationship. Moreover, although the impact of leisure reading habits on reading competency would be difficult to isolate, most people—educators, parents, and students themselves—would agree that reading for pleasure should be encouraged.

When one high school teacher asked her students to write histories of their reading experiences, she found a common thread: an enthusiasm for the world of books in the earlier grades, which faded with adolescence. Many students attributed this decline in enthusiasm to the rigid structure of their classes. One student wrote:

> Before I could read, I was always having stories read to me by my family. And when I became capable of doing it myself, well, I kept on going. I have just recently cleaned out my closet and found some rather large boxes filled with books. These books were children's books and the odd thing about all of this is that I recognized every one of them . . .

I loved them all, the puppies, the chicks, the fire engine, Willy-Woo-Woo, and many more.

It is hard for me to remember anything about elementary school and the reading while I was there outside of one thing, the Hardy Boys. I read every Hardy Boys mystery novel imaginable. That is the only recollection of reading that I have from my elementary days through about the seventh grade. The Hardy Boys were my passion. I would just read forever. In fact, many of the books I read four or five times.

In eighth grade, everything seemed to change. Now we were actually forced to read, and I don't like to get forced to do anything, especially in school. In English we read *Lord of the Flies*, *1984*, and another one of George Orwell's masterpieces, *Animal Farm*. That took up my reading time in that year of school. One vital point is that I became burned out; since I could not read these books at my own pace, it lowered the enthusiasm I had for reading.

As I continued on to high school I did not do an ounce of reading outside of school. Although I am an avid reader of exotic car magazines, I don't believe that really counts. I did not do any reading besides what was assigned to me in school classes, and I didn't read those half the time, either (Sullivan 1991, 41-42).

Research involving a variety of student types has documented the trend of decreasing interest in reading as students mature. For example, a cross-sectional study of gifted secondary school students found that younger students report more reading activity than older students, and more interest in reading for fun (Anderson, Tollefson, and Gilbert 1985). A study of low-income students in grades three, six, and nine found that younger children held more positive beliefs about reading than older students (O'Sullivan 1992). Compared to students in the sixth grade, those in the ninth grade reported that reading was more difficult, less interesting, and less enjoyable. A study of middle school students found that almost three-fourths of them reported reading less than one hour daily on a regular basis; 20 percent had read only one book for pleasure in the last six months (Lesesne 1991).

On a broader scale, although the influential 1985 report *Becoming a Nation of Readers* underscored the importance of leisure reading to reading development, no increase in leisure reading has been observed in the years since this report was released. In fact, the percentage of 17-year-olds who reported reading for fun on a daily basis was lower in 1996 than in 1984, and the percentage who reported never reading for fun was higher. This study indicates that there might be a pattern of decreased reading for fun as students age: whereas 54 percent of 9-year-olds reported in 1996 that they read for fun on a daily basis, only 32 percent of 13-year-olds and 23 percent of 17-year-olds reported these leisure reading habits (National Center for Education Statistics 1997).

❖ STUDENTS AT RISK OF READING FAILURE ❖

For some students, the problem is much more severe than a declining interest in reading. Students at risk of reading failure in the middle and high school years are likely to have already experienced failure in school and to have low literacy skills. Such students may have learning disabilities, may just be starting to learn English, or may merely be reluctant readers who have not mastered grade-level reading skills. Demands in the higher grades for content-area reading competency create continuing problems for these students, with reading deficiencies negatively affecting many other areas of school performance.

Past failures with reading, and with school in general, typically result in low levels of motivation. However, it is with these students—who need to be actively engaged—that the most *un*motivating techniques are often used. Remedial reading courses are often taught at the students' present level of functioning, with emphasis on basic skills rather than the importance of reading for meaning. In compensatory or remedial classes, students may spend a large portion of their time in passive activities such as completing worksheets (Allington and McGill-Franzen 1990; Carbo 1994). This is not to say that basic skills instruction is unnecessary; in some cases it is essential to specifically address a student's weak area. In fact, direct instruction in reading components such as phonics and word identification can be quite successful (Chall and Curtis 1992). The potential danger, however, is that it may become the focus of remediation efforts, at the expense of providing students with real reading tasks and motivating them to enjoy reading.

An interactive approach to reading instruction might include high-interest reading materials, the opportunity to discuss readings in small groups, reading aloud, or student dramatization of plays. Recently, researchers have focused on "reading styles," and evidence suggests that the reading comprehension of poor readers can be improved by matching instruction to their reading styles (Carbo 1987). The reading style of poor readers can often be characterized as global, tactile, and kinesthetic. That is, they need hands-on experiences with reading materials, including activities like computer-assisted instruction and role-playing; also, materials should be of high interest and involve these students emotionally (Carbo 1994).

The importance of an interactive approach is underscored by other research with at-risk learners. For example, a reading workshop with elements such as self-selected texts and journal responses was found to improve the reading skills of at-risk ninth- and tenth-grade students (Kletzien and Hushion 1992). This approach highlights reading as an enjoyable activity, which is especially important; these students will not become life-long readers unless they perceive the reading process as enjoyable (Carbo 1994). The importance of using an interactive approach with at-risk students was expressed well by one middle school remedial teacher:

> My students there taught me as much as I taught them, and their strongest lesson was a frightening one: adolescents who have not been successful—have failed—in traditional classrooms are at risk. Unless we find ways to engage them, they will shut down. If we continue to focus only on identifying deficits and devising sterile remedies, these students will surely use their energy and talent for unproductive purposes—or not at all (Krogness 1995, 1).

All students need engaging activities to truly be turned on to reading, but at-risk, remedial readers are particularly in need of an interactive approach.

LIMITED TIME FOR IMPLEMENTING READING STRATEGIES

Class size, pressure to cover content, and lack of planning time are all constraints teachers experience when they want to set aside time for teaching reading strategies or activating student interest in reading. This is particularly true in the case of the content-area teacher. Because of such time constraints, teachers must continually make individual determinations not only about the *effectiveness* of any given strategy, but also about its *efficiency* as well.

Any procedure used must be efficient in terms of time and payback. The primary focus should be on strategies that work well—that is, strategies that encourage higher levels of learning for *all* students, while recognizing the particular needs of those students who are most at risk for reading failure. Support from the school's reading specialists is also critical. Unfortunately, secondary schools frequently do not provide this kind of support.

BUILDING ACTIVE READERS ACROSS THE CURRICULUM

Given that reading is a critical concern for those dealing with middle level and high school students, what is the major purpose of secondary school reading instruction?

In its policy resolution on adolescent literacy, the International Reading Association contends that adolescents entering the "adult world" today will need to perform more reading and writing tasks—and contend with a greater flood of information—than at any other time in human history (International Reading Association 1999). Therefore, the overriding goal behind any reading strategy should be to foster active, engaged, independent readers. In recent years, approaches to reading instruction have focused on the constructive nature of reading. That is, the meaning of a text is not contained within the printed words themselves, but rather arises from the reader's interaction with the text. The reader actually creates meaning by synthesizing the material with his or her background knowledge and personal experience. The strategies described in this book are intended to put readers in an active role, while improving reading skills and increasing motivation to read.

This report addresses reading in the content-areas as well as reading in the English classroom, providing a number of strategies that both content teachers and English teachers can use to improve reading skills and enhance interest in reading. Although English can certainly be considered a content area with its own subject matter, the term "content area" will be used in this report to refer only to non-English classes (subjects such as social studies, math, and science). The term is used in this way because opportunities for reading instruction and reading-related activities can often be structured more easily into the English classroom than into other subject areas. Therefore, the kinds of issues that English teachers and non-English teachers face regarding reading instruction are, in some cases, quite different. Moreover, the research itself makes this distinction. Yet despite the differences, these two areas also contain similarities, which will become more apparent as the topic is addressed.

Motivational Factors
Related to Reading

Motivational factors play an important role in reading habits, preferences, and achievement level, and thus should be an important consideration when planning reading instruction. Five major motivational factors will be discussed: developmental needs during adolescence, attitude towards reading, interest in reading, the effects of television, and parent involvement.

❖ ADOLESCENT DEVELOPMENTAL NEEDS ❖

By examining some of the developmental needs that characterize adolescence, reseachers have identified issues critical to developing responsive, effective secondary reading instruction. Adolescents need opportunities for:

- *Self-exploration and definition.* Adolescents need to explore their new cognitive and linguistic abilities, and to consider how they might use them in their future adult roles. Providing free reading periods in which students choose their reading, as well as having students write personal responses to text in a dialogue journal, are good ways to facilitate self-exploration.

- *Competence and achievement.* Adolescents often feel unsure of themselves. Assessment of literacy achievement, therefore, should focus on providing information on student progress, rather than simply judging academic successes and failures.

- *Diversity.* Teenagers vary greatly in their interests and abilities. Teachers should allow not only for diversity in reading material, but also for different types of class activities, ranging from quiet, independent work to social interaction in literature discussion groups.

- *Physical activity.* Adolescents tend to need more physical activity than is provided in the typical intermediate or secondary level classroom. A workshop-like setting that includes literacy activities ranging from individual writing to paired or small-group work and large-group discussion, in addition to teacher lectures, can provide opportunities for movement and activity (Davidson and Koppenhaver 1993).

One middle school teacher describes how she took advantage of adolescents' distinct developmental needs to get them involved with literature:

> How do adults help thirteen- and fourteen-year-olds harness their energy, sublimating all those new and arresting drives so that they can be still long enough to learn? Although no secret formulas exist, I tried to use the qualities—being provocative, challenging authority, finding their own individuality, seeking justice, and believing in their own immortality—that set eighth graders apart as a way to hook them on to language learning. I chose to tap rather than to fight those peculiar tendencies. I tried to capitalize on eighth graders' desire to be in charge of their lives. By design I connected the special projects we did, the formal debates we had, and the literature we read with the temperament of rapidly changing adolescents (Krogness 1995, 49-50).

This teacher selects texts that grapple with themes central to adolescence. Such themes abound in young adult books, such as the theme of disobeying authority in Robert Cormier's *The Chocolate War*. Although young adult books are often viewed as light reading materials that are not of the literary quality of the "classics," they allow adolescents to bridge the gap between the childhood reading materials and the classics. Young adult literature in the classroom will be discussed in more detail in Section Three.

❖ INTERNAL INFLUENCES ❖

Reading achievement is not just a matter of reading ability; it also can be significantly affected by how students feel about the activity of reading and about themselves as readers. The roles that factors such as student attitude toward reading and student interest in reading play are of increasing interest to researchers and practitioners.

ATTITUDE TOWARD READING

There is a strong relationship between reading attitude and reading comprehension. For example, O'Sullivan (1992) examined what she termed "students' motivational beliefs about their reading ability"—beliefs that they could "take control of their reading, set high standards, and achieve their goals." She found that the beliefs of her subjects (low-income students in grades three, six, and nine) significantly influenced their reading achievement. Further, these student beliefs were heavily influenced by the beliefs of teachers and parents.

Because of the relationship between reading attitude and reading comprehension, assessing students' attitudes should be a part of any class that includes reading. Ways to assess attitude include:

- *Questionnaire.* This might include such questions as: How do you feel about reading? Do you consider yourself a reader? If not, what don't you like about reading? Do you consider yourself a writer?

- *Reading autobiography.* Each student writes a personal history of his or her reading experiences.

- *Portfolio.* This consists of a student's responses to individual texts.

- *Letter of intention.* Students write letters to themselves at the beginning of the school year, stating what they hope and expect from the year to come (Krogness 1995).

INTEREST IN READING

Degree of interest in reading material has also been linked to comprehension. Studies involving low-achieving secondary students (Belloni and Jongsma 1978) as well as higher-ability fifth- and sixth-grade students (Stevens 1980) found that pupils comprehend material better when it is more interesting to them. Theoretically, these effects *could* be attributed to background knowledge rather than to interest, since subjects in which we are interested are often those about which we have prior knowledge. However, one study separated the effects of interest from those of prior knowledge, and the researchers found that even when separated, there were significant effects for both prior knowledge *and* topic interest (Baldwin, Peleg-Bruckner, and McClintock 1985).

There are a variety of ways to find out more about the individual interests of students. For example, students can fill out interest inventories—questionnaires or checklists that make the teacher aware of common interests among students. The teacher can then assign reading materials that involve these common interests. If thematic units are part of the curriculum, the inventories can be used as sources for topic ideas. Or, students can interview each other about their interests and report them to the teacher. Teachers should also keep abreast of general teen reading interests; lists of teenagers' favorite books are readily available. For example, such a list is published every year in the *Journal of Reading*. This list is compiled by giving adolescents from sample schools around the country a large list of books published within one particular recent year; the adolescents then vote on their favorite books.

EXTERNAL INFLUENCES

Environmental factors such as television and parental role modeling can exert a powerful motivational influence as well. While these factors may seem to be minimally within the control of the school environment, there are several effective ways that educators can address them, such as encouraging students to be informed and critical television watchers, and promoting parent involvement in school.

THE EFFECTS OF TELEVISION

One common concern among educators, parents, and others is that television negatively impacts students' academic achievement, especially their reading skills. A review of the research on the relationship between television viewing and reading achievement found these negative effects (Beentjes and Van der Voort 1988):

1) When children spend time watching television, that activity is replacing other activities such as homework and reading.

2) Watching television promotes passivity because it does not require much mental effort.

3) Due to the rapid, continuous pace of most television programs, TV reduces a child's ability to concentrate.

When weighing the potentially harmful effects of television, one issue to consider is the amount of time spent per day on this activity. The authors of the study described above conclude that detrimental effects on reading achievement may occur only among children who watch four to six hours of TV per day. Another more recent study found that, at all three grade levels tested (four, eight, and 12), students who reported watching three or fewer hours of television a day had higher average reading scores than their peers who reported watching four or more hours a day (National Center for Education Statistics 1999). Both of these findings argue for the importance of limiting TV watching.

In a more positive light, television has been used successfully in secondary classrooms as a powerful teaching tool (Lawrence et al. 1993). Used appropriately, instruction using television not only capitalizes on the strong interest that many adolescents have in this medium, but it also provides an opportunity to think critically about the subtle messages embedded in television programs. Examples of projects include: studying the propaganda techniques used in advertising; evaluating the quality of television journalism (in light of the recent upsurge in "tabloid television programs"); and analyzing PBS programming.

Parent Involvement

Studies involving younger children reveal that those who like to read for fun have parents who model reading (Morrow 1983), in addition to encouraging their children to read (Neuman 1986). Surveys of adolescents reveal important findings that build on this relationship. A study of 13- and 17-year-olds' reading practices found that those students who reported infrequent reading activities in their home had lower reading proficiencies. The same study found that students with higher reading proficiencies had more books in the home and more home literacy resources such as dictionaries, atlases, and computers (National Center for Education Statistics 1997).

Research also tells us that parents of successful secondary readers know about the school's reading program, visit their children's teachers, and are more likely to participate in school programs (Lutz 1986).

Suggested ways to get parents involved include:

- *Project Bookshelf:* Post announcements in school bulletins and newspaper press releases, encouraging parents to go through their bookshelves and look for appealing books to donate to classroom libraries.

- *Parent tutors:* Recruit parents to tutor reading skills. Parents may be volunteers, or they might be paid through grant funds; they should be provided with training about the school's reading program and about techniques for teaching reading.

- *Reading advisory board:* Create a board composed of teachers and parents to explore how teachers and parents can work together to improve the reading program.

- *Bookstores/book fairs:* Schedule book fairs on weekends or when parents are in school for another activity. A book fair can include a variety of activities and displays, such as information booths, films, computer learning booths, student book reviews, reading games, read-a-thons, and book giveaways.

- *Reading awareness week:* The week might include activities such as visits from local authors, including parent authors. Teachers can send home lists of recommended books, tips on selecting books for adolescents, or bookmarks.

- *Parent book talks:* Invite parents to come to the classroom and give book talks to students.

- *Book discussion groups:* Invite children and their parents to select books from a list, read them, and discuss them in informal groups in the classroom. Afterwards, children and parents could exchange letters about their book sharing experience (Morris and Kaplan 1994).

- *Family literacy programs:* Family literacy programs are designed to work with parents and their children (typically at the preschool level or in the early grades) for the purpose of improving the literacy development of the children or the entire family. Programs might include parent literacy education, support groups for parents, or opportunities for planned interactions between parents and children (Morrow, Tracey, and Maxwell 1995). Generally, adolescents are included in family literacy programs only when they are the parents; however, these programs might also be beneficial for at-risk adolescent students from families with low literacy skills.

It becomes especially important to communicate with parents about the school's program when implementing some of the newer classroom approaches to instruction and assessment, such as portfolios. To actively involve parents, one teacher asked her students' parents to experience portfolios first hand (Robbins et al. 1994). The parents were asked to prepare a reflective analysis about their child, which would contain information about the personal background of the student and learning goals that the student should set for the year. Parents responded in a variety of creative ways, such as letters, videos, and essays. The teacher found that this kind of exercise helped parents understand her instructional goals, and it fostered greater home support of the reading program.

Approaches for
Actively Engaging Students in Reading

In recent years, curriculum reform efforts have focused on the need to actively engage students in learning. Hallmarks of an interactive reading program include:

- Students play an important role in suggesting or selecting reading materials.

- Time is set aside during the school day for students to read silently or aloud.

- Classrooms have an abundance of print materials.

- Students have an opportunity to respond to reading material (such as literature, newspaper articles, and biographies) in writing—for example, by writing in dialogue journals.

- Students discuss their reading materials in small groups.

- Students draw on personal experience in order to understand what they are reading.

The principles listed on the previous page are all components of *whole language theory*. The whole language approach emphasizes the importance of natural learning situations in which language is dealt with in context, and in which meaning making is considered the central focus of reading and writing (McWhirter 1990). It is especially important that students read and write about things that interest them. Because natural learning situations are central to this theory, whole language research relies more on naturalistic observations such as case studies than on quantitative evaluations (Goodman 1992).

Although the whole language approach is usually discussed in the context of the elementary grades, a study of two teachers and four English classes reveals the advantages of implementing an interactive approach to reading at the secondary level. The teachers were given guidance about interactive reading methods, but also were free to choose which methods they wanted to use, based on their own understandings and preferences. The teachers subsequently modified their teaching styles and established small groups for literature discussion, assigned students to write joint essays on literary topics of their own choosing, and incorporated student suggestions in lesson plans. Teachers reported that they had revitalized themselves and their classrooms; students read more and expressed more interest in what they read (Gross 1991).

ENCOURAGING STUDENTS TO READ MORE AND READ WIDELY

Instructional strategies such as dialogue journals and small-group discussions about reading material are excellent ways to engage adolescent readers. However, before these strategies are examined, the focus will be on strategies that can simply encourage students to read more—in both their English classes and their content-area classes. Again, the more students read, the better they read. What kinds of reading materials and reading environment create a classroom that turns students on to reading? This section will take a look at factors that can increase reading activity and, subsequently, the enjoyment of reading. These factors include: providing choice in reading materials, establishing a print-rich environment, including light reading and young adult literature in the curriculum, exposing students to a wide variety of materials, making time for in-school free reading, reading aloud, and designing thematic units.

CHOICE IN READING MATERIALS

Instead of requiring the entire class to read a particular book, teachers can provide students with a list of books from which they choose the titles that most appeal to them. It is critical that this list be designed with student interests in mind. Results from Kellerman's (1991) study suggest that when student interests are not taken into account by those selecting books for independent reading, students reject the books. Kellerman writes: "Only four out of the fifteen books chosen by teachers for free reading assignments matched the students' top six preferences in terms of interest [areas]. The remainder of the books were among the students' least preferred types of books" (14-15). Moreover, case study research clearly indicates that students prefer being able to select their own reading (Gross 1992; Kletzien and Hushion 1992; Carlsen and Sherrill 1988).

CREATING A PRINT-RICH ENVIRONMENT: CLASSROOM AND SCHOOL LIBRARIES

Research also supports the assertion that when books are readily available, more reading is done (Krashen 1993). Collections in classroom libraries or schoolwide library media centers help to get adolescents excited about the world of books. These libraries could be set up in content-area classes as well as English classes; content-area classroom libraries could contain a supply of light reading materials relating to the subject under study. Atwell (1998) contends that not only does a classroom library invite readers to browse, chat about books, and be selective about their choices, but it also demonstrates that reading is a high priority to the school.

Classroom libraries should contain a wide array of high-interest materials such as young adult novels, historical fiction, and science fiction books. Research indicates that classroom libraries are often designed with insufficient attention to student interests: a study of middle school students' reading preferences and access to reading materials found that students had limited school access to their preferred reading materials, such as scary books, comics, and magazines about pop culture. In fact, classrooms ranked a distant last for book sources, even for students from low-income families (Worthy, Moorman, and Turner 1999).

Classroom library materials should represent a wide range of reading levels, because struggling readers will improve their skills through opportunities to read materials with 95 percent word recognition accuracy (Ivey 1999). "High/low books" (high interest/low vocabulary materials) are particularly appropriate for struggling adolescent readers; several bibliographies of these materials are available (e.g., Phelan 1996). Picture books are also a valuable addition to the classroom library. Such books are appealing to many early adolescents, provide reading practice for struggling readers, can offer a rich cultural diversity of stories and artwork, expose students to advanced vocabulary, and work well as an introduction to abstract topics because they activate background knowledge and stimulate curiosity (Miller 1998).

A national study of high school literature programs examined the role of the school library and found that good libraries *do* make a difference to the literature program (Applebee 1993). Applebee compared school libraries in award-winning schools with those in a random sample of public schools. (Award-winning schools were drawn from a sample of schools that had consistently produced winners in the NCTE Achievement Awards in Writing Program; most of the 88 schools chosen were public. The random sample of 331 public schools was nationally representative.) This study found that there are three vital components to a good school library: collection size, accessibility, and title availability.

- *Collection size.* Award-winning schools report a greater number of volumes available, yet no difference is found in terms of per-pupil statistics. This suggests that *per-pupil calculations may not be as critical as sheer collection size,* as one researcher who reviewed these findings speculates: ". . . this may be a case in which statistics obscure rather than enlighten. Students and teachers don't experience a library on a 'per-pupil' basis. More volumes available is simply that—more volumes in a collection that can be devoted to literature topics proportionately" (Burroughs 1993, 163).

- *Accessibility.* An accessible library is one that has extended hours (perhaps open before and after school, or on weekends), is open to the general public, and contains resource-sharing networks (such as inter-library loan programs). Upon reviewing research on library accessibility, Krashen (1993) concludes that access to school libraries, larger library collections, and longer library hours all result in more reading.

- *Title availability.* Schools in Applebee's survey were asked whether or not their library held 24 specific titles. Included on the list were works of literature by women and minority authors, as well as young adult books. Award-winning schools had far more of these titles (19 out of 24) than did the random sample of public schools (13 out of 24).

Young Adult Literature in the Classroom

The types of reading that typically appeal to adolescents include teen romances, comics, science fiction, and problem novels (novels with teen characters who have realistic problems, such as dealing with divorce, puberty, or alcohol abuse). These books stand in sharp contrast to the literary canon prescribed in the curriculum of some secondary schools, which includes such classics as *Hamlet*, *Of Mice and Men*, and *The Scarlet Letter* (Applebee 1993) and excludes works such as Cormier's *I Am the Cheese* and L'Engle's *Ring of Endless Light*. More and more, however, teachers are realizing the value of bringing young adult literature into the classroom, for these books have the potential to spark interest in even the most reluctant readers. One obstacle to incorporating these books into the curriculum is that teachers rarely have complete freedom over the literature they teach. The great majority, however, have at least some leeway and may add materials to the core selection or ask to have additional selections approved (Applebee 1993).

Contrary to prevailing beliefs, the term "young adult literature" is not synonymous with low-quality literature. In fact, a few of these works have even managed to establish themselves in the secondary curriculum—for example, *Lord of the Flies* and *The Outsiders* (Applebee 1993). Eighth-grade teacher Nancie Atwell writes:

> The last thirty years have witnessed an explosion in the volume of novels and short stories written expressly for young adults, adolescent literature of breadth, depth, and power. Much of the writing—I'm thinking of Robert Cormier, Sharon Creech, Walter Dean Myers, Elizabeth Berg, Madeleine L'Engle—is both exquisite and profound. More importantly, much of the sentiment expressed in contemporary adolescent fiction mirrors and celebrates . . . emerging power—that sense of independence and self—of the adolescent mind. As adults can turn to fiction for portrayals of the universalities of our condition, so our students can find their perspectives reflected and explored in a body of fiction of their own, books that can help them grow up and books that can help them love books (1998, 36).

Adolescent literature has several additional benefits. Enriching the school library's light reading collection is an effective way to bring students into the library, thereby promoting reading in general (Krashen 1993). Especially compelling is the evidence that light reading can serve as a conduit to heavier reading. A poor reader will, at least initially, select materials that are congruent with his or her skill level; this light reading provides students with the motivation and the reading skills that make more difficult reading possible. A review of the research shows that many children who do extensive free reading eventually choose what experts have decided are "good books," and they expand their reading interests as they read more (Krashen 1993).

Reed (1985) contends that young adult literature responds to the developmental needs of adolescence, acting as a bridge between the books of childhood and the books of adulthood. The themes of young adult literature correspond to the egocentric, identity-seeking themes of adolescence; most teenagers are not yet fully ready to appreciate literature for its aesthetic value. One researcher who interviewed adults about their adolescent reading experiences noted the detrimental effects of assigning the classics too early: "Some . . . revealed that they were absolutely baffled by the classics, which are assigned, today, as early as the sixth grade. Others professed shame that they found them dull as teenagers and really liked mysteries and adventure stories better. Some respondents withdrew completely from the world of books because the classics were so far beyond their level of reading ability" (Carlsen and Sherrill 1988, 154).

However, reading light materials exclusively will probably *not* lead to advanced reading skills, because reading ability is related to reading materials—whereas good readers prefer abstract, imaginative, and complex material, poor readers prefer material that is more concrete (Hafner, Palmer, and Tullos 1986).

EXPOSURE TO A WIDE VARIETY OF MATERIALS

Although an awareness of adolescent reading interests and the interests of particular students is important—with many reluctant readers needing high-interest, low-level reading material to motivate them to read—the concern that students *broaden* their interests must also be addressed.

The approach used by a teacher can make a difference. One teacher emphasizes student responsibility to generate interest by giving students a page of the telephone book to read for 10 minutes, then asking them to note how they tried to bring interest to the material (Oritz 1983). As students become aware of the techniques for bringing interest to material, they will begin to realize that a book's degree of interest is in part reader-generated, rather than an absolute.

Some other tips for broadening interests:

- Provide reading material in the classroom that reflects a wide range of interests and reading difficulty.

- Invite local authors to talk about books they have written; also invite parents or community members to share special interests or hobbies, and try to link these interests to books in the school library.

- Use movies to stimulate interest in different subjects, and introduce books that relate to these subjects.

- Have students give "book talks" about the books they are reading to small groups of students. A successful book talk program includes the following: teacher modeling of book talks, establishing heterogeneous groups of five to six student book talkers, and dramatic oral readings of exciting passages (Moscrip 1991; Eldridge 1998). Students giving book talks in content-area classrooms might select biographies of renowned historical figures or scientists, current events articles, or works of fiction that either recreate a historical period or bring a content-area concept to life.

Educators should not only be concerned with diversifying students' reading *interests*, but also with diversifying the *types* of materials that students read. For example, in a social studies classroom, students might read newspaper articles, stories about people from different cultures or times, or travel guides in addition to the textbooks. In English classes, the concern with diversifying reading materials focuses on exposing students not only to novels, but also to materials such as plays, poetry, and biographies. The importance of this factor is underscored by research involving teacher experience. One study found that experienced content teachers are less likely to depend on the textbook to structure their lessons than are relatively unexperienced teachers; for example, less-experienced teachers often rely on text information for lectures or discussions (Menke and Davey 1994).

Recent research findings call attention to the need to diversify reading material for younger students: NAEP's 1996 study found that, "according to the reports of 9 year olds, fewer students were reading poems and plays in 1996 than in 1984" (National Center for Education Statistics 1997, 135). However, more positive data from the study show that when compared with 1984, greater proportions of 13 year olds in 1996 were reading both poems and plays, and that 17 year olds in 1996 were reading more biographies and science books (135).

IN-SCHOOL FREE READING

Time available for reading is also a factor to consider. In interviews with adults who recollected their reading experiences, many spoke of decreased time for leisure reading during adolescence (Carlsen and Sherrill 1988). In the teenage years, opportunities for new activities abound, such as clubs, dating, sports, music, and social events; at the same time, the homework load is likely to increase. Regrettably, all of these activities take time away from pleasure reading. Perhaps the only way to encourage adolescents to read for fun is to set aside time for free reading during the school day. Moreover, making time for students' independent reading serves as a demonstration that reading is a high-priority concern to teachers and schools.

In an in-school free reading program, the teacher, or even the entire school, sets aside a certain period of time during the day or week in which students can read books of their choice. Students can select material from the school library or from the classroom bookshelf, or even bring in reading of their own choosing. It is essential that teachers read silently along with the students, rather than using the time to complete paperwork. Following the reading period, teachers may ask students to write in response journals about what they have read. One 11th-grade English teacher describes implementing a "saturation reading" approach for six weeks in the semester, with procedures in place to check whether reading has been done and to assess comprehension of the material read (Leighton 1991). However, many advocates of free reading caution against holding students accountable for what is read, because that will discourage a reluctant reader.

To be most effective, free reading programs should include all readers, low- and high-achieving alike. It is, in fact, *low-achieving readers* who most need assessment-free opportunities in order to develop the lifetime reading habit. Ironically, though, these students are far less likely to be assigned silent reading than are high-ability readers (Davidson and Koppenhaver 1993). Although the primary focus of a free reading program is not to develop reading skills but to develop reading *habits* and encourage students to become life-long readers, improvement of reading and writing skills is often a by-product. Specifically, Krashen (1993) documents positive effects of reading on vocabulary, writing style, and spelling.

READING ALOUD

Reading aloud is a common activity in elementary schools. Research supports the notion that this activity is crucial for elementary school children, indicating that children who are read to at home read more on their own and demonstrate increased comprehension, vocabulary, and interest in reading (Krashen 1993).

However, many secondary school teachers view this activity as a time waster that is not suited to adolescents (Ecroyd 1991). On the contrary, oral reading by a teacher can provide an opportunity to model reading, demonstrate one's own excitement about literature, and get teenagers enthused about literature. This anecdote provided by an English teacher conveys the motivating power of oral reading:

> Last year, a student who knew that I had cut the narrative between the grandfather and grandson, wanted to read all of William Goldman's *Princess Bride*. Similarly, when I read John Gunther's *Death Be Not Proud*, several students checked out the book so they could read the letters and

Francis' entry at the end—which I had edited out in my oral reading. Thus, reading aloud can successfully motivate students to read on their own (Ecroyd 1991, 77).

Also, oral readings of classics such as Shakespearean plays can be instrumental to generating interest in classic literature (Carlsen and Sherrill 1988).

Guidelines for a read-aloud program for teenagers include:

- Read the book first, to be sure that it is something you like and want to share with others. Although students may not like everything you like, they won't be interested in a book if you aren't.

- Select passages that are powerful (suspenseful, gory, hilarious, or romantic).

- Before beginning the read-aloud session, relate the work to something the teenagers know about.

- Stop reading before students stop listening—the oral reader should constantly monitor the interest of listeners and their body language. At the first sign of boredom, either move on to another activity, increase the drama in your voice, or skip some passages to get to the good parts quickly.

- Give listeners an opportunity to respond to what has been read, and emphasize the importance of a nonthreatening atmosphere while they are responding (Matthews 1987).

Reading aloud is especially beneficial for at-risk students. It can provide these students, some of whom have never finished a book, with the sense of enjoyment that comes from reading and completing a book. A secondary teacher who works with at-risk students tells of the benefits of oral reading:

> Everyone loves to hear a good story. Because many of the kids hadn't been read bedtime stories by their parents when they were little, my reading *Home Before Dark* or sometimes telling them parts of a story fulfilled several needs: it allowed us to start class quickly and it invited everyone to settle down and settle into language, to savor the easy rhythm of the story setting, and to picture the characters. Listening to the book made reading seem accessible to these young people, who often declared themselves nonreaders (Krogness 1995, 144).

An effective approach to reading aloud in the content-area classroom is Rapid Retrieval of Information, or RRI (Green 1998). Students begin by reading the text silently in class. Then the teacher poses questions that require recall as well as higher-level thinking skills such as drawing inferences and analyzing. Students skim the reading to search for answers, and the teacher calls on volunteers as well as non-volunteers to read aloud the words or paragraphs that contain the answer the question. Green writes: "The combination of using higher level thinking skills, scanning information, and reading aloud highly motivates most of my students" (1998, 307). Additionally, RRI provides the teacher with valuable diagnostic information regarding students' decoding skills, fluency, comprehension, and ability to skim information.

❖ TALKING ABOUT TEXTS ❖

When we think about the activity of reading, the image that comes to mind for most of us is that of a solitary reader curled up in a chair, engrossed in a book, oblivious to the rest of the world. Yet, reading is rarely a purely solitary phenomenon. Even when we read a book by ourselves, it is often in a social context, such as in a classroom, a library, or at home in the presence of family members, where a potential exists for sharing the reading experience. Books can serve as a catalyst for social interactions between the reader and others. For example, one might select books based on a friend's advice or analyze a text with others who have read it. Adolescents experience the social aspect of reading through activities such as joining book clubs, discussing teen romance novels during lunch periods, and picking up the books that a sibling has checked out of the library.

A wide assortment of activities that highlight the social nature of reading can be introduced in the classroom, such as book talks (see page 20), group projects as part of a thematic unit (see page 34), and small-group discussions.

SMALL-GROUP DISCUSSION

Small student groups assembled to discuss works of literature (or other reading materials) can be highly effective in enhancing reading comprehension and interpretation, as has been shown in studies involving both elementary and secondary students (Sweigart 1991; Nystrand, Gamoran, and Heck 1993; Strickland et al. 1989; Eeds and Wells 1989; Leal 1992). One study found that students are aware of how text-based discussions help them understand what they read. Students reported that discussion allowed them to become engaged with ideas, construct meaning, and take responsibility for their own learning (Alvermann et al. 1996). Furthermore, this type of learning strategy has been found to be superior to lecture or whole-class discussion in facilitating the understanding of complex ideas (Sweigart 1991).

It is important to note, however, that in order to be effective, small-group work must be carefully designed. One element that seems to affect the instructional effectiveness of small groups is the amount of autonomy that students receive. Nystrand, Gamoran, and Heck (1993) compared the effects of different types of small-group work on achievement in the study of literature, and they found that autonomous groups (in which the students in the group define and resolve the problem) are more effective than problem-solving groups (in which students are required to come to a consensus about a problem defined by the teacher), which are in turn more effective than "collaborative seatwork" (an activity highly structured by the teacher, such as completing worksheets in a group). The authors recommend that teachers design small-group assignments that specify the parameters of the activities, yet allow the students themselves to determine the precise nature of the activities. In Alvermann et al.'s 1996 study of middle and high school students' perceptions of text-based discussions, many of the students expressed the opinion that a certain degree of student autonomy was critical. One of the themes that emerged was that good discussions center around a mutual exploration of ideas rather than following teacher guidelines, and that students' agendas might be different from the teacher's intentions but nevertheless productive and relevant to the content at hand.

Nystrand, Gamoran, and Heck advise teachers to keep in mind that, while small-group discussions are particularly appropriate for certain educational goals, they are less appropriate for other goals. There are times when a lecture-style class format may be more appropriate, such as when a great deal of new information is being introduced. Worksheets may be appropriate at times when the teacher wants students to practice a newly developed skill. But, as the authors write, "If teachers want students to compare ideas, develop a train of thought, air differences, or arrive at a consensus on some controversial issue, then the forum of small groups may be just the right setting for most students to carry on intensive conversation" (1993, 22).

Benefits of small discussion groups include:

- These groups take advantage of the social nature of secondary students.

- A high proportion of students speak in carefully designed discussion groups. One researcher found that 90 percent or more of students spoke during a student-led discussion format (Knoeller 1994).

- Discussion groups are instrumental in developing skills such as cooperation, inquiry, problem-solving, and communication.

- Students who participate in these groups do more than just receive information; they are also placed in the role of expert or resource. The implicit message is that developing their own thoughts, and not just remembering someone else's, is important.

- When reading independently, struggling readers often make irrelevant associations that interfere with comprehension. Such learners need to hear other viewpoints and compare them to their own thinking to improve their understanding (Collins 1996).

DESIGNING SMALL-GROUP WORK

When first establishing the small-group discussion format, teachers are often concerned about whether or not students will talk, if one student will dominate the discussion, or if students will have difficulty keeping the conversation focused on the text. Here are some tips for designing and supporting discussion groups:

- Group size should ideally be between four and eight—large enough to bring diversity of opinion, but small enough to ensure that all students can participate fully (Wiencek and O'Flahavan 1994).

- Groups should consist of students with heterogenous abilities. Make a chart rating the social, interpretive, and reading abilities of each student in your class, and place students in heterogeneous groups based on these abilities.

- Rearrange groups until you are comfortable with them, and ask students whether the groups are acceptable to them.

- Accept that not all discussion will be focused on higher-level thinking. Sometimes enthusiastic conversations that are only superficially related to the text serve the purpose of providing an "easy entry into the discussion" and putting teenagers in an "active, evaluative role" (Roller and Beed 1994).

- How often should groups be changed? Seek students' advice on when they see the need to rearrange groups, but keep in mind that since students need time to establish their group dynamic and interactive norms, the initial changing of groups probably should be delayed six to eight weeks. However, if a group isn't working out at all, you may want to disband it and have members join the remaining groups (Wiencek and O'Flahavan 1994).

Scott (1994) suggests that the assignment of roles to students in literature discussion groups can provide a helpful framework for encouraging students to focus on different facets of the reading process. In a framework developed by Scott, each student assumes one of the eight roles; if the groups have fewer than eight students, the roles most fitting the work of literature should be used.

The eight roles are:

- Discussion Director—Designs and discusses questions about the text.
- Passage Master—Notes and shares important passages.
- Connector—Makes connections between the book and real life.
- Illustrator—Illustrates and shares an important part of the story.
- Scene Setter—Tracks and describes the settings in the story.
- Character Captain—Responds to the actions of the characters.
- Word Wizard—Defines and discusses interesting or confusing words.
- Summarizer—Briefly summarizes the key points.

These role structures could also be suitable for non-fiction materials. For example, a group discussing a science article or textbook chapter could potentially use the roles above, with the likely exceptions of Scene Setter and Character Captain.

One way to promote autonomy in small discussion groups is to encourage students to conduct independent research after discussing topics that are of great interest to them. For example, when one teacher designed literature circles around social issues such as child abuse and war, some students still had so many questions after the discussion that they were motivated to extend their own learning through interviews and research. In this approach, students directed their own learning and explored answers to questions that were important to them (Noll 1994).

USING DISCUSSION GROUPS WITH AT-RISK AND REMEDIAL READERS

Discussion groups are particularly appropriate for at-risk and remedial readers. Too often, these students are viewed simply by their weaknesses, and it is assumed that the personal experiences they bring to the classroom have no merit (Gentile and McMillan 1994). Discussion groups call upon the firsthand knowledge of these students to interpret a text, underscoring the value of their personal experiences.

When designing small-group work for at-risk students, some modifications are likely to be necessary. Shorter amounts of text may be more appropriate than a whole book for a reading assignment. If the students have had little experience with small-group instruction, teachers should specifically address the ground rules for conducting a discussion when introducing the activity. In addition, the teacher might work with the entire class at first, until students acclimate themselves to the activity; students might then be divided into smaller groups for discussion of the reading (Gentile and McMillan 1994).

To help remedial readers develop their discussion skills, teachers must do more than simply pose questions for students to answer. An effective technique is to initially model both questions and answers, which provides remedial readers with critical exposure to comprehension processes and clarifies the discussion task. After ample modeling, teachers can gradually diminish the support and transfer responsibility to students (Curran 1997).

Note Cue is a method that provides students with support in their initial attempts to participate in discussion groups (Manzo and Manzo 1990). It is suitable for any students who seem to be struggling, including students who speak English as a second language. Note Cue tells students *what* they might say in class discussion, leaving them only to think about *when* they should say it. The advantage of this strategy is that it "builds behaviors by first producing an appropriate behavior where previously there were none, or only inappropriate ones" (609).

To implement Note Cue, the teacher gives students notecards that contain teacher-developed questions, answers, and comments that might be made during discussion of a particular text. The teacher then invites pupils to first read questions, then answers that might fit the questions, and then fitting comments. The students must decide at what point in the discussion their contributions are appropriate. The reading of teacher-prepared notecards may seem like mindless parroting, but in fact it has the potential to make students feel more competent, in that they develop situationally appropriate behaviors for discussion participation. The strategy includes specific ways to gradually foster the learner's independence—for example, the teacher could write suggestions on the notecards that students ask certain kinds of questions, such as questions that raise doubt.

COOPERATIVE LEARNING GROUPS IN CONTENT-AREA CLASSROOMS

One way of incorporating cooperative learning groups into the content-area classroom is to create reading strategy groups (Montague and Tanner 1987). Students first learn several reading strategies, such as SQ3R, the Directed Reading-Thinking Activity, and the "Click or Clunk" strategy (see pages 42-45). Next, students evaluate the benefits of each strategy by completing a brief questionnaire. Students are then assigned to reading strategy groups consisting of four to five individuals who have chosen the same strategy. Each group develops its own guidelines for group participation; some groups will decide to use the strategy together and produce a single written product, while others will choose to assist one another in using the strategy to produce individual papers. Montague and Tanner write, "Emphasis is placed on interactive content learning where group members actively question one another, validate what they know through discussion, and organize new information using the strategy as the framework" (721).

Gauthier (1989) suggests a number of guidelines for reading groups in the content areas. Before forming the groups, first limit the amount of text to be read at one time—it should ideally be only a short selection. Activate prior knowledge and introduce key vocabulary. Then, ask students to read the selection and write responses to these three items: 1) *What have you learned from reading this selection?* 2) *How does the information in this selection connect to the other things you know about this subject?* and 3) *List the words in the selection that you do not fully understand.* After the students discuss these questions in small groups and write their responses, the teacher should join in the discussion, either by moving from one group to another, or by assembling the students in a whole-class discussion.

CULTIVATING THE READING-WRITING CONNECTION

Most people would agree that there is a strong connection between reading and writing, and that what we read influences our choices of writing topics, as well as the genres of our written work and our writing style. Research into the relationship between reading and writing confirms this assumed connection: that is, those who read well often also write well (Smith and Dahl 1984). This phenomenon has been explained in several ways. It has been suggested that writing contributes to a reader's sense of the author's craft, and of the strengths and weaknesses of literary works (Tierney and Leys 1986). In addition, skilled reading and writing have both been linked to reflective behaviors and metacognitive awareness (Birnbaum 1986).

In secondary classrooms, writing is most often used for evaluative purposes (Sensenbaugh 1990). Another potential, yet often overlooked, function of writing is to help students learn material. For example, a recent study of 11th-grade English students found that understanding of a story was enhanced when followed either by formal analytic writing (in which students used textual evidence to support their arguments) or by personal analytic writing (in which students explained and elaborated on their personal responses to the story) (Marshall 1987). Those who wrote responses to short-answer questions scored lower on a post-test than those who did extended writing. These results point to the importance of giving students opportunities to compose extended written responses to their reading materials, either in the form of text analysis or in the form of personal reactions.

The term *writing* actually refers to a variety of activities. In-school writing might mean any of the following: writing a summary of a textbook chapter; expressing oneself personally in a dialogue journal; writing an essay; revising a draft of a paper; or editing a peer's work. Moreover, writing can be integrated with reading in several different ways. Writing might be a pre-reading activity (such as jotting down associations with the Ice Age before reading about it), or a post-reading activity (such as analyzing the structure of a Robert Frost poem).

WRITING AS A PRE-READING ACTIVITY

Pre-reading activities increase student engagement with reading material by activating what students already know about a topic. The reading-writing connection can be emphasized by asking students to write down prior relevant knowledge before reading about a topic. For example, in individual or group brainstorming sessions, students might make associations with the concepts they will read about. As an alternative, students could write down their personal thoughts or experiences that relate to the topic. Autobiographical writing before reading increases understanding of a text, engagement in discussion, and under-standing of characters; also, students who write before reading stories tend to like the stories better (White 1992, 1995). This technique could be used as easily in any content-area classroom. For example, when beginning the study of geom-etry, the teacher could ask students to write down some things they already know about shapes.

DIALOGUE JOURNALS

A dialogue journal is an informal, written conversation between a student and another person (usually a teacher, but it could also be a peer or parent), in which participants chat, either about issues of importance to them or about the material they are reading. Benefits of using dialogue journals include:

- Students have an opportunity to write for a genuine audience.

- Teachers have one-on-one time with students that otherwise might not be feasible.

- Dialogue in these journals has the potential to go beyond the parameters of usual classroom discourse because the conversation is more private, and those who are shy or unsure about the value of their own ideas express themselves more readily.

Dialogue journals are an effective way to get students involved with their texts, because the goal of such journals is not to write polished essays, but to express honest responses to texts and to become more aware of the reading process without having to worry about elements such as grammar and punctuation. The benefits of dialogue journals are underscored by a case study of two veteran English teachers who introduced them in their classrooms (Gross 1992). Both teachers found that the students enjoyed this activity, became more eager to read, were more engaged in reading, and liked sharing ideas with peers.

Guidelines for students who write in reading dialogue journals include:

- Express your personal responses to reading—your opinions, feelings, likes, and dislikes.

- Relate the book to your own experiences; write about similar things that have happened to you.

- Don't worry about spelling and grammar. Expressing your thoughts is more important.

- Talk about things you don't understand, or ask questions about what is happening or why something is happening.

- Make predictions about what will happen in the rest of the book. As you continue reading, keep track of which predictions came true, but don't worry about being wrong.

- Praise or criticize the book, giving specific reasons why you feel this way, such as the writing style or subject matter (Fuhler 1994; Wells 1993).

Because teachers are flexible about grammar and other language rules when reading the dialogue journals, those students who are not native English speakers may feel more free to write than they might when given other writing assignments. Students speaking very little English could even draw pictures to express their ideas, to which teachers might respond initially with pictures and a few words. Dialogue journals can also provide opportunities for exchanging cultural knowledge between people of different nationalities.

Journals may be used in conjunction with an independent reading program, as a forum for discussing books students have chosen. Conversations can be recorded in a notebook (preferably a spiral bound one, in order to resist wear and tear). At the back of the notebook, students can keep a log of what they have read and when they completed a reading. This serves as an easy reference for teachers, readers, and parents.

Students should write regularly in dialogue journals—ideally at least once a week. Because dialogue journals require regular reading and responding from teachers, time management is an important concern. Keep in mind, however, that dialogue journals are not simply an added demand on teaching load. In fact, they can *replace* some kinds of written work, as one middle school teacher asserts:

> I remember suffering through piles of junior high book reports, the dullest writing I've ever read. By contrast, the [kids'] letters are a constant source of surprise, pleasure, and stimulation. And what they replaced—book reports, worksheets, quizzes, and tests—ate up more time than keeping up with my correspondents ever will (Atwell 1998, 298).

Students should have the opportunity to write to diverse audiences, such as peers and parents. It has been found that students write different kinds of journal entries to peers than to teachers; for example, students are more likely to recommend books to one another than to teachers (Wells 1993), and they write more often about their emotional reactions to a book when writing to a peer (Atwell 1998). In addition, involving parents in the dialogue journal process is a powerful way to link home and school (Fuhler 1994).

THE READING-WRITING CONNECTION IN THE CONTENT AREAS

There are several ways to foster the reading-writing connection in the content areas. The time investment for these activities may seem great, but it can pay off by providing teachers with valuable information on how much their students comprehend, as well as by increasing student engagement with the text. Some suggestions are (International Reading Association 1990):

- *Journal writing.* Set aside time at the end of class, perhaps five minutes, for students to engage in this activity. Teachers might ask pupils to write in their journals about their own classroom learning experiences, to explain concepts in their own words, or to pose questions.

- *Free writing.* This pre-reading strategy invites students to describe what they know about a topic before studying it. Following this brainstorming session, students could share their ideas with the rest of the class.

- *Creation of possible sentences.* This technique is a tool for making meaning from technical vocabulary and content-area concepts. Teachers first display key vocabulary that is defined in a passage to be read; students use key vocabulary to predict sentences that may appear in the lesson and then read the lesson to verify the sentences they have written, evaluating them for accuracy and correcting errors.

❖ **OTHER APPROACHES** ❖

Interactive approaches to reading instruction might also include structured classroom debates and thematic units; these types of activities often call upon students to use critical thinking skills in interpreting their reading materials. Using computers to promote reading instruction is a relatively new approach that, when carefully designed, can be highly effective.

CLASSROOM DEBATE

Teachers often avoid provoking academic conflicts among students, either because such conflicts are perceived as divisive, or because an instructional model is not readily available. However, structured classroom controversies have been shown to result in greater student mastery of the subject, an increase in the quality and number of ideas, creative insight, and student enjoyment (Johnson and Johnson 1988). Moreover, in-class debate is particularly well suited to adolescent learners, as noted by these researchers:

> Teenagers have a natural propensity toward questioning, challenging, and arguing as they seek to establish who they are, what they believe in, what they want to accomplish, and what they expect from life. This process of moving from strong parental influence to the more powerful peer influence is a very active one. Teaching methods that acknowledge and capitalize on this stage of human development can be very effective. ... One such method that gets students actively involved in discussing literature is debate (Schauer and Beyersdorfer 1992, 57).

Opportunities to debate could be provided in the content-area classroom in a number of ways. For instance, students could debate environmental issues in science class, take the sides of political candidates in social studies class, or even debate the uses and misuses of statistical polls in math or social studies classes, with some written material suggested by the teacher as source documents. The four steps listed below provide one possible structure for designing student debates:

1) Introduce the class to the idea of a planned controversy and the need to resolve it; remind them of the importance of respecting opinions different from their own.

2) Establish a background for the controversy. Ask students to read textbooks and primary source materials.

3) Determine which side each student will be on. Students may take the side they actually support, or they may be randomly assigned. Remind

students that a good debater can argue for either side of an issue. Ask students to find evidence for their side in the material they have read.

4) Involve students in a simulation where they are forced to take a position on the controversy. The format for the debate might include opening statements, presentation of arguments, rebuttals, and closing statements. If a winner is to be chosen, ask observing students to keep track of which team presented more arguments that were not successfully rebutted by the other team (Schauer and Beyersdorfer 1992).

This approach not only requires reading by the students, but also demands that they process what they read in a way that utilizes higher order skills.

THEMATIC UNITS

In a thematic unit, a topic or theme provides the focus for study. Thematic units can be implemented in *all* the content areas. In fact, themes often come from the fields of science or social studies—examples of topics include the American Revolution, weather, and the life cycle. Themes that most interest adolescents include those that grapple with difficult issues, such as the effects of technology on society (Weaver 1994). The advantage of a thematic approach is not only that it integrates various areas of a discipline by relating them to a theme, but also that it lends itself to using a wide range of reading materials written at different difficulty levels. A wide variety of activities, varying from individual written work and small-group creative projects to in-class dramatizations, can be incorporated in this approach.

For example, a thematic unit on the American Revolution could include activities such as creating a timeline of pictures depicting major events of the American Revolution, acting out the courtroom scene from the novel *Johnny Tremain*, writing letters to the editor either for or against the Boston Tea Party, or producing a classroom edition of the *Boston Observer* newspaper as it might have appeared during that period (Weaver 1994).

Thematic units can vary in the extent of student involvement. When students have a major role in planning the thematic unit—identifying main ideas and finding resources—they feel a sense of ownership of the project and are more likely to invest themselves in the process of learning (Weaver 1994). Greater student participation in the planning does not, however, mean that teacher responsibility for planning is lessened. In fact, shifting more responsibility to students often requires that a teacher be more organized, in order to ensure that the learning potential provided by the activity contributes to the unit's goals.

Another way of structuring reading activities within a thematic unit is to assign students to read one book together as a class and allow each student to self-select another related book. To guide students in choosing relevant books, the teacher can design a list of texts, keeping student interest in mind. After the teacher introduces the books by providing brief information on each one, each student chooses a book and reads it in class. This approach is called Guided Independent Reading; Podl (1995) reports that the student choice component fosters a sense of ownership and pleasure in reading.

READER'S THEATER

Readers can enhance their understanding of story characters and plot through the technique of Reader's Theater. One way of approaching Reader's Theater is for students to assume the roles of characters and pantomime the character's personality and emotions, perhaps reenacting important conversations between different characters. Students could also take roles and read the text aloud as a script, using their vocal expression and discourse style to recreate the characters. After the Reader's Theater performance, classmates could discuss whether the reenactment reflected their own understanding of the characters and plot, referring to the text itself to support their interpretation. This approach gives students an important opportunity to practice reading toward a goal (Curran 1997; Ivey 1999).

CONCEPT-ORIENTED READING INSTRUCTION

Concept-Oriented Reading Instruction (CORI), developed by the National Reading Research Center, begins with real-world observation, which creates motivation and sets the stage. For example, students might observe the plant and animal life in a park, handle fossils, visit a historical landmark, or build a replica of a Native American totem pole in their classroom. If this real-world observation sparks curiosity, students will read, write, and discuss their observations and reflections with enthusiasm. The curiosity will then develop into a set of personalized questions, which the students can seek to answer through reading relevant books in the classroom library. After retrieving information, students integrate the resources into coherent answers to their questions and communicate the answers to the rest of the class (Guthrie, Alao, and Rinehart 1997).

The CORI approach emphasizes a wide variety of reading strategies during all stages of the activity, such as notetaking, skimming, summarizing, activating prior knowledge, and identifying main ideas. Teachers are actively involved in helping students use these strategies as tools to help them reach their goals.

COMPUTERS AND READING INSTRUCTION

With the advent of the information age, computerized instruction has begun to play a critical role in our schools, and several studies have shown that computers can be useful and motivating tools for reading instruction.

The effectiveness of computer-assisted reading instruction depends largely on the type of computer programs used. The most effective programs are those that provide students with whole texts, foster active involvement, or include opportunities for learners to make decisions that influence the computer task—rather than "locking" teachers and students into drill-and-practice exercises that emphasize isolated language fragments (Simic 1993).

Well-designed computer-assisted reading instruction can offer several important benefits (Wepner, 1990; Divine and Whanger 1990; DeGroff 1990):

- It gives students a sense of control.

- Students enjoy graphics and animation.

- Students often report that working with the computer is fun, and that they are motivated to read.

- Students can progress at their own rate, separate from the pace of the rest of the class.

- Students experience immediate reinforcement for their work.

- Computers provide opportunities for social interaction, either through pairing students up at computers or through use of telecommunications.

- When students can communicate with others via tools such as electronic mail, they have a real purpose for writing and reading, and a real audience.

- Computer-assisted reading instruction can reduce fear of failure and so be especially helpful for at-risk adolescents.

One example of a computer program that has been successfully used with secondary students is Baggetta_Ware, which leads students through classics that are broken down into small, more manageable segments. After the software displays a segment, it asks students to answer questions about material they have read, scores their responses, and displays the next segment. The interspersing of questions between the text segments prompts students to pay careful attention to what they are reading, and the interactive element is engaging (National Education Association 1999). Baggetta_Ware can be run on computers with Windows 95 or 98. At this writing, the Web site to access for more information is http://baggetta.click2site.com.

Another feature that computer-assisted instruction might include is hypertext, a method that links on-screen information to other information, allowing users to select which links to follow and which concepts to explore. Students can access information in a way that feels natural to them, rather than following a specified path. A case study of an American history class provides a step-by-step description of how one teacher was able to successfully design a hypermedia program to instruct her students in history (Dillner 1994). This teacher designed a computerized lesson on the Bill of Rights, which, through the use of hypertext, allowed users to choose which of the items to read (for example, which amendments to learn about in-depth), as well as what assignments to complete. The advantage of this program is that it allows each student to read about a content area in a nonlinear fashion, and in an order that is interesting and comfortable to each individual.

Another approach to using computers to increase reading skills was adopted by a school district in North Carolina. Student gains on a reading achievement test, over a period of five years, were reported after a computerized reading management and enrichment program was implemented (Peak and Dewalt 1994). Students first chose and read books from a list of 900 works of classic literature, then took an individualized test on a computer. The computer tracked their reading progress and generated reading reports for teachers, parents, and students. The program was carefully designed: it accommodated a wide range of reading levels, it was noncompetitive in nature, tests were motivational as well as instructional, and students were able to read and be tested at their own pace. The researchers compared the scores of students at a school that implemented this program with the scores of students at a similar school in the district that did *not* implement the program. Not only did they find that the program significantly increased reading achievement, but they also found that it increased the number of books read per week, and that a majority of students liked the approach.

Computer-assisted reading instruction can also be implemented with simple word processing software. For example, one way to help students extract meaning from texts is to teach them how to color code word-processed texts for meaning. Students might select different colors for different types of sentences and phrases, such as topic sentences, opinions versus facts, or descriptions versus narratives. If color coding is done on the computer rather than with highlighter pens, students will have the opportunity to reconsider and redo their coding, and then possibly print out their final result on a color printer (Viau 1998).

With the proliferation of web sites, many educational materials that can be used to supplement texts can be found on the Internet. To help ensure that students comprehend what they are reading, a set of guided questions about the text can be prepared and provided to them. The set of questions could be put on diskette, and the students could then move back and forth between the Internet and the word-processed questions to search for and type in answers (Lewin 1999).

Computers can also provide a highly motivating approach to connecting reading and writing in the curriculum. For example, one teacher made the text of a passage available as a computerized document, and then gave students guidance in specific ways to manipulate the text on the computer screen, such as adding their own thoughts and questions, or reorganizing the concepts within the material (Bernhardt 1994). This approach encourages interaction with the material, and gives readers a sense of ownership. An important point—with all these approaches just discussed, teacher planning and guidance is the key to whether the approach provides worthwhile opportunities for student learning.

Metacognition:
Developing Good Reading Strategies

Good readers demonstrate an ability to use certain kinds of strategies that are termed "metacognitive." Metacognition refers to the awareness of one's thinking processes, and the ability to regulate, evaluate, and monitor them. For example, a metacognitive strategy that good readers might use before starting to read would be considering their prior knowledge about a subject and identifying the purpose for their reading. During reading, strategic readers: monitor their comprehension (perhaps by paraphrasing the material, checking the accuracy of predictions they have made, or asking themselves questions to see whether they understand); recognize obstacles to comprehension (such as unusual writing style, too many unknown words, and lack of background information); and try to remedy problems in comprehension when they occur (perhaps by rereading the passage or changing reading speed).

Because the strategic reader is continuously checking his or her level of comprehension and filling in any gaps, metacognitive strategies facilitate active, engaged reading. Interestingly, although strategic readers are highly aware of their thinking and reading processes, their approach to reading is often implicit, and they may not be aware that what they are doing would be termed a "metacognitive strategy."

Poor readers—or, more generally, poor learners—demonstrate much lower levels of competence with metacognitive strategies. Even when attending to the mechanics of the task at hand, they may have little idea of the reasons for doing it, how to approach its solution, or how their efforts relate to outcomes. This lack of understanding of the learning process may present an even greater barrier to learning than deficits in some of the basic skills needed for a particular content area. On a more positive note, students can be taught good reading strategies if they are explicitly explained, modeled, and regularly incorporated into classrooms (Helfeldt and Henk 1990; Smith 1992). Once learned and applied, they are tools that can be used in situations both inside and outside classrooms. As such they should also be considered valuable *products* of the learning process.

Some of the basic skills that underlie metacognitive strategies are:

- *Predicting.* Predictions encourage students to read with a purpose and to confirm or correct their predictions as they construct meaning. One strategy that uses prediction is the Directed Reading-Thinking Activity (see page 45).

- *Self-questioning.* Self-questioning allows learners to actively check how much they understand while reading. Students can pose questions such as *What is the main idea?* and *Are there examples to help clarify the main idea?* Students who generate their own questions have been shown to have greater improvement in comprehension than students who simply answer questions posed by teachers (Singer and Donlan 1982). A number of specific self-questioning strategies have been developed, such as SQ3R (see page 44).

- *Paraphrasing.* By putting the concepts of a passage or section in their own words, or by summarizing the main points, students can get a sense of how much they understand.

- *Visual representation.* Creating visual models of ideas within a text provides a means of organizing information into understandable wholes, and promotes the visualization of relationships (see pages 45-46).

- *Lookback.* This strategy involves referring to what has already been read in order to increase understanding of the material.

- *Changing reading speed.* When students encounter obstacles like an unusual writing style or too many unknown words, they can modify their reading speed. Also, good readers are able to determine the appropriate pace for their purpose. For example, they can determine when it is best to quickly scan the material (frequently useful when reading the newspaper, for example), and when material is best approached with slow and deliberate reading (such as a complicated math problem).

PRE-READING ACTIVITIES

Three important objectives of pre-reading activities are:

1) to get students to think about what they already know about a topic;

2) to direct their attention to a purpose for which they will be reading; and

3) to spark their interest and curiosity in the topic (Ciborowski 1992).

Types of pre-reading activities that teachers might implement include:

- *Oral previews.* Components include: short questions and statements designed to catch the students' interest and provide a link between a familiar topic and the story's topic; story synopsis; introduction of characters; and definition of unfamiliar words. Oral previewing has been shown to improve both story comprehension and recall (Graves, Cooke, and Laberge 1983).

- *Introducing core vocabulary.* Students will encounter new words and terms in their reading (particularly if they are reading in a content area). An introduction to the most important vocabulary terms makes the reading more approachable and gives students an idea of what the reading will be about.

- *Autobiographical writing before reading.* Students can write down their own personal experiences that relate to the topic. Autobiographical writing before reading enhances understanding of the text (White 1992), as well as engagement in discussion and understanding of characters (White 1995).

- *Writing down predictions.* Students predict what they think they will learn; after reading the text, they write what they actually did learn.

- *Anticipation guides.* Students answer five or more teacher-prepared true-false statements about major concepts within the topic they are about to study. These guides can motivate reluctant readers if they include controversial statements or statements that challenge students to examine their beliefs. Student responses will help the teacher determine which misperceptions need to be corrected in the course of study; this is an important step in enhancing students' comprehension (Barton 1997).

- *Drawing analogies.* When students lack important background knowledge, teachers can use analogy as an interpretive bridge between unfamiliar material and what students do know. Hayes and Tierney (1982) found that using analogies as a pre-reading strategy improves students' recall and prediction skills.

- *Brainstorming about initial associations with key concepts.* This activity has been found to improve story comprehension (Langer 1984).

When instruction helps readers activate prior knowledge, attention becomes better focused on a reason for reading. Ciborowski (1992) writes that "reading becomes more gratifying because its purpose is now more apparent" (34). In fact, setting a purpose for reading is critical to good reading skills. Langer (1993) studied the approaches to literary understanding among secondary readers, and concluded that what sets better readers apart from poorer readers is a tendency to think about the primary purpose for reading. Poorer readers lacked "a vision of the kind of knowledge they are after in the first place" (36). One way to focus on the purpose for reading is to use the KWL strategy, in which students make lists of what they Know, what they Want to know, and then what they Learned (Ogle 1986).

USEFUL STRATEGIES DURING READING

Numerous strategies have been developed to help readers monitor their comprehension, and new strategies are continually being developed. Several examples of comprehension strategies are described below. It is important to introduce only one or two reading strategies at a time, when earlier ones have been internalized. Mastery of any of these strategies may take several days of practice or longer.

"CLICK OR CLUNK" STRATEGY

This is a particularly useful strategy when working with nonfiction. At the end of a section of reading, students should ask themselves if the meaning of a text "clicks" for them or if it goes "clunk." If it clunks, they should ask what they can do to make sense of it. Weaver (1994, 157) writes: "This is a delightfully simple yet effective way of getting readers to stop their reading and rethink rather than continuing to read without comprehension. It is most likely to be adopted by students if the teacher repeatedly demonstrates how he or she uses it, and teachers and students use it collectively."

RECIPROCAL TEACHING

The reciprocal teaching strategy, developed by Palinscar and Brown (1984), calls upon teachers and students to take turns asking each other questions about the text. Reciprocal teaching might occur as students and teachers read a passage of material, paragraph by paragraph. During the reading, they frequently take time out to ask each other questions and monitor their comprehension.

There are two phases to this strategy. The first step is instruction in the use of four comprehension-monitoring strategies: summarization, question generation, clarification, and prediction. This means that at first, the teacher assumes most of the responsibility for instruction. In the second phase, however, the students begin to take on more responsibility—they begin to ask questions, request clarification of material they don't understand, make predictions about what will happen next, and summarize what they have read (Rosenshine and Meister 1994).

The reciprocal teaching strategy offers several advantages to learners. Because students can witness what questions the teacher thinks are worth asking, they have a model available for the questions that they themselves will formulate. Through using this strategy, students discover information sources for questions and develop the habit of self-questioning. In addition, students are put in the unique position of being able to assume a teacher role. This contrasts sharply with the more traditional student role of answering questions that are posed in the text or by the teacher.

Teachers might enhance students' reading comprehension by pairing reciprocal teaching with an intervention called Paragraph Patterns (Spiak 1999). Science teachers in one school found that when reciprocal teaching was first introduced, most students speed-read through the material and did not remember the concepts well. To hold students more accountable for what they read, the teachers implemented Paragraph Patterns, an approach that involves identifying and writing down the main idea of a paragraph. Content comprehension scores more than doubled after the intervention, and students were better able to identify the main idea of passages.

SQ3R

This is a well-known strategy that involves skills such as summarizing, self-questioning, and text lookback. There are five steps:

- *Survey*: Skim a chapter for general understanding before reading it.

- *Question*: Formulate questions using the chapter's boldface headings.

- *Read*: Read a section to locate answers to the questions that have been formulated.

- *Recite*: Paraphrase main ideas and supporting details, and check them against the passage.

- *Review*: Recall main points before reading subheadings; recall as much supporting information as possible (Call 1991).

SCAN & RUN

This instructional framework consists of cues for strategies that help students plan and monitor their comprehension before, during, and after reading expository text. Instruction in the use of SCAN & RUN has resulted in higher scores on homework, quizzes, and tests for low, average, and high achievers; moreover, both teachers and students expressed high satisfaction with this strategy (Salembier 1999).

Before reading, students use four SCAN cues while previewing chapter text:

S = Survey headings and turn them into questions (students will answer the questions during the reading).

C = Capture the captions and visuals (reading the captions and looking at the visual clues to try to understand what each means).

A = Attack boldface words (reading boldface words, which are usually key vocabulary words, and figuring out what they mean).

N = Note and read the chapter questions (reading the questions at the end of the chapter so that they can be kept in mind while reading the chapter).

While reading the chapter, students use the three RUN cues:

R = Read and adjust speed (adjust reading speed depending on the difficulty of the section).

U = Use word identification skills such as sounding it out, looking for other word clues in the sentence, or breaking words into parts for unknown words.

N = Notice and check parts you don't understand and reread or read on (place a check mark next to the part you don't understand, and decide to reread that section or skip it and go back to it after you're finished reading).

After reading, students extend their understanding of the text by answering questions at the end of the selection and discussing the text.

Instruction in the use of SCAN & RUN involves several steps that facilitate independent use of the strategy by students. Instruction begins with a whole-class introduction to the strategy, followed by teacher modeling of a think-aloud process to illustrate how to use each SCAN & RUN cue while reading a chapter from the course text, encouragement that students memorize the seven cues through round-robin rehearsal games, and student completion of a self-monitoring chart of their use of SCAN & RUN cues.

DIRECTED READING-THINKING ACTIVITY

The task of a Directed Reading-Thinking Activity (DR-TA) is to generate hypotheses about the material to be read, then refine these hypotheses while reading. A DR-TA is a powerful tool for fostering independence in readers, because it encourages them to use their reasoning abilities and tap their own knowledge. There are four steps to this activity:

1) *Predict.* In this stage, students reflect on what they think will be covered in the text. These predictions are recorded on the board, on an overhead projector, or on charts the students create.

2) *Read.* Students then read a few paragraphs or pages of the text.

3) *Confirm.* Students compare the predictions they made with what was actually presented in the text. (Steps one through three are repeated until the text is completed.)

4) *Resolution.* Students summarize and evaluate the text (McIntosh and Bear 1993).

VISUAL REPRESENTATIONS

The strategy of developing visual representations of thinking processes (such as causal chains, webs, and if/then flow charts) has become popular in recent years. These kinds of visual depictions are intended to keep students focused on content and to clarify the learning task. In addition, they momentarily freeze the learning process so that students can observe the process itself. They can be highly effective learning tools; one district reports that after visual representations were introduced, student scores on a state reading test increased dramatically (Peresich, Meadows, and Sinatra 1990).

When using this strategy, teachers need to carefully consider what kind of representation to employ for a specific task. Different visual representations support different ways of thinking about a topic. For example, time lines help students arrange events chronologically; web diagrams help them tie related ideas to one concept; pro/con charts help students weigh evidence; and if/then flow charts let them work out steps in deciding between two or more choices. If the teacher first perceives and conceptualizes the material to be presented or read, he or she can determine the most appropriate visual approaches. However, part of the training in the use of visual representations should focus on developing student independence in deciding which method to use.

Visual representations are an excellent way for teachers to check what students already know about a topic and how well they understand the key relationships and issues. They can be used before, during, and after reading, and they are a useful study strategy that allows teachers to correct misunderstandings before formal assessment occurs. Furthermore, developing visual representations can become a cooperative learning activity, with small groups working together.

EMBEDDED QUESTIONS

If questions are embedded in a narrative or expository text, followed by blank lines where students can write or draw their answers, they help to interrupt ineffective reading processes and prompt students to actively work to comprehend a passage. Students might be prompted to describe the setting, make a prediction, write a question, or summarize. Students also might mark up the text by highlighting evidence to support inferences, unfamiliar vocabulary, or words that establish the mood.

The embedded questions approach offers several benefits for learners: it gives students experience in annotating and manipulating text, promotes independent work with a text, and lays a foundation in comprehension that enables students to participate in substantive discussion of the reading. Furthermore, a carefully sequenced, guided implementation of embedded questions has been shown to increase students' awareness of metacognitive strategies and improve reading comprehension scores (Weir 1998).

INSERT

INSERT was developed by Vaughn and Estes (1986) as a method for readers to recognize when their comprehension breaks down, and to encourage students to focus on new or important information within a text. It is particularly useful in situations where students own their books and are free to mark them. If this is not the case, students can simply attach post-it notes to the margins of their books. The instructor should write the following symbols on the board, and ask students to copy them:

Marking system for INSERT

X	I thought differently
+	New information
!	WOW
??	I don't understand
*	Very important

Allowing students to invent their own symbols is another technique that can be used to heighten interest in the approach and encourage its use.

STORY MAPS

Story maps are graphic organizers with headings that are names of story elements, such as setting, problem, events, and resolution. These headings prompt students to locate key information from the story during or after reading, and write the information down. Research has shown that story maps help students develop a sense of story structure, which in turn improves their reading comprehension. Teachers first model story mapping by thinking aloud, locating information in the text, and writing down the information under the appropriate heading. The modeling process should include specific self-instruction statements, such as "As I read, I am finding and listing story elements so that I can understand what happens next," which helps students understand the purpose of the strategy and how to execute it (Swanson and De La Paz 1998).

SOME THINGS TO KEEP IN MIND WHEN TEACHING METACOGNITIVE STRATEGIES

Incorporating metacognitive strategies into the curriculum involves more than teaching a set of techniques. While introducing strategies, teachers need to:

emphasize the underlying purposes of using them, address obstacles students face when trying to learn them (such as ineffective techniques they may already be using), and actively promote strategy use (model it and link strategy use to learning outcomes).

MAKE SURE LEARNERS UNDERSTAND A STRATEGY'S PURPOSE

Metacognitive strategies have the potential to increase students' reading skills, although educators must be aware that a strategy becomes a metacognitive tool only if its purpose is understood. For example, a student can only make good use of a visual representation strategy such as a web if he or she realizes that creating a web is a tool for thinking about and recording the relationships between different text elements. If the student does not approach it with this in mind, the web is simply an assignment—an extra piece of busywork to complete. While efficient learners may implicitly know how to use metacognitive approaches as tools, others may see no tie between the web and their efforts to learn content unless they receive special instruction.

DISMANTLE INEFFECTIVE ROUTINES

Results from Garner and Hare's (1984) study on text lookback provide a cautionary note for those teaching reading strategies. These researchers found that while text lookback (referring to what has been read in order to better understand) worked with middle school students, it did not work with high school students. They suggest this might be because junior high students are generally lookback novices, whereas some high school students have already acquired lookback techniques that are not effective. Therefore, older learners may need to dismantle ineffective routines before they can assimilate effective routines.

MODEL THE USE OF A STRATEGY

When introducing specific metacognitive strategies in the classroom, teachers should first model usage of the strategy. For example, a teacher might model prediction by thinking out loud: "The name of the chapter is Effects of Climate on Culture. I know that some places in the world are better for farming than others. Will this chapter talk about how communities in places like this are different from those that get almost no rain?" Bonds, Bonds, and Peach (1992, 56) would describe this example as a "model of how one monitors, questions, and recalls what is to be learned."

To facilitate student independence, teacher support should be gradually diminished. After the teacher provides several examples of thinking aloud while applying a strategy, students could take turns applying the strategy with help from the teacher and classmates, either in large or small groups. With this practice, students will eventually gain competence in performing the tasks independently (Curran 1997).

LINK STRATEGY USE TO LEARNING OUTCOMES

Results from a recent study highlight the importance of motivation to strategic learning (Chan 1994). Findings indicate that students who believe they have control over their learning outcomes and who have a positive image of their academic abilities are more likely to use strategies in their learning. The author asserts that the findings "support the need to provide students with strategy instruction and to convince them that learning outcomes are attributable to the use of strategies" (336). Teachers may even find it useful to conduct an in-class demonstration that provides evidence that strategy use can improve learning.

Other Techniques
to Improve Reading Skills

In addition to the metacognitive strategies described in the previous section, other techniques are available to teachers for improving students' reading skills. Two techniques are described below: vocabulary development, which is essential to reading development in general; and peer tutoring of reading skills, an alternative instructional strategy that is supported by research findings.

❖ VOCABULARY DEVELOPMENT ❖

Two kinds of vocabulary development are fundamental to secondary schools: 1) general vocabulary development, which is typically included in the English curriculum and may, for example, call upon students to study a pre-selected list of words every week; and 2) content-area vocabulary development, which involves teaching the language and concepts associated with a particular subject area.

As important as these two areas are, approaches to vocabulary development often relegate students to a passive role. When students are given teacher-prepared vocabulary lists from which they must look up and memorize definitions, not only do they become turned off to reading, but they also do little meaning-making. Words in pre-selected vocabulary lists often lack connections to the real world or to the student's own reading. One study found that when students are put in a more active role (for example, rather than simply writing out definitions, they combined several definitions into one meaningful sentence), their performance on a subsequent vocabulary test is better (Santa 1988).

Here are some other suggestions for making vocabulary assignments more active:

1) Students receive a photocopy of an article chosen by the teacher or by a classmate. The teacher first underlines a few specific words that students should learn, and then asks students to select other words they don't know. Students write out guesses of the meanings for all the selected words, look them up, and choose the dictionary meanings that fit their context (Ianacone 1993).

2) The Vocabulary Self-Collection Strategy (VSS) (Haggard 1986). There are two varieties: the VSS for general vocabulary development, and the VSS for content-area vocabulary development.

For general vocabulary development: Each student, as well as the teacher, brings to class a word that he or she believes the entire class should learn. Learners should find words in their own environment and determine their meanings as best they can from context (they do not necessarily have to look up the word). Learners share the word with the class, the class adds information to the definition, and then the entire class agrees on a definition. A class word list is compiled by including student-selected words, excluding those words most students know and those that students choose not to learn at that time. At the end of the week, students are tested on the class word list.

For content-area vocabulary development: The primary purpose in this case is to learn content, so students should be looking for words that will help them do so. After completing the assigned reading, students work in groups of two or three to identify words that are important for learning lesson content. The teacher then writes these words on the board, and student teams provide a definition from the context. Class members add any additional important information; the class then goes about creating a class word list, using the process described in the previous paragraph.

3) IT FITS, a strategy based on keywords, can provide struggling readers
    with critical support in vocabulary development. Students first write the
    word and its definition on an index card (Identify the term and Tell the
    definition). Next, students Find a keyword they know that will help
    them remember the vocabulary word and write it on the card. Then they
    Imagine and Think about a connection between the vocabulary word
    and the keyword, and draw a picture on the card to help them remember
    that connection. Finally, students Study the card until they have memo-
    rized the definition. For example, if the vocabulary word were "biomes"
    (large land areas where specific animals live), the student would write
    the word and its definition on the card. The student might select the
    keyword "homes" to remember this definition and write it down. To
    illustrate the connection between the words, the student might draw a
    nature scene where animals are enclosed in homes (Lebzelter and
    Nowacek 1999).

PEER TUTORING

Peer tutoring in reading has been shown to improve the reading skills of
both the learner *and* the tutor (Topping 1987; Pickens and McNaughton 1988).
This strategy involves one student helping another student (or a small group of
students) with lower academic skills, in a program that is structured and super-
vised by a teacher. Peer tutoring is a cost-effective way of dealing with the
problem of too few teachers, and it also takes advantage of the power of peer
influence.

Some other benefits of peer tutoring include:

- Tutees get individual attention they might not otherwise receive; they
  often identify better with peer tutors than with adult authority figures;
  and they receive immediate clarification of material they do not understand, in a nonthreatening environment that is optimally free of criticism
  and competition.

- Tutors get a chance to be leaders and assume responsibility, which helps
  build confidence and self-esteem. By explaining the subject matter to
  others, peer tutors come to understand it better themselves.

- Adolescents usually like tutoring because of its active and interactive
  nature.

- Teachers have more time to work with those most in need of assistance.

SOME GUIDELINES FOR ESTABLISHING A PEER TUTORING PROGRAM

Many elements of reading can be incorporated into a peer tutoring program—word recognition, identifying story structure elements, and metacognitive skills such as text lookback (Rekrut 1994). Research suggests that peer tutoring is most successful when teachers provide structured lesson plans for tutors to follow (Jenkins and Jenkins 1987), when specific skills are taught, and when responses are easily determined to be correct or incorrect (Miller et al. 1993).

Before taking on their roles as tutors, students should first be trained in interpersonal skills (helping without giving the answers, providing encouragement), as well as management skills (allocating time for tasks, measuring and recording student performance). Students should also be made aware of issues such as punctuality and confidentiality, as well as the purpose of the tutoring program itself.

Researchers suggest assigning tutors to same-sex partners for comfort and modeling reasons (Rekrut 1994). Tutors and tutees need not be in the same grade level; they are often several years apart in age, which is referred to as "cross-age tutoring." In the secondary school, students in the upper grades who have already successfully completed a class might tutor those in the lower grades. Another option is for secondary students to tutor elementary students; this activity is particularly well-suited to low-achieving secondary students, who can then review basic skills while being in a high-status role, and therefore will not perceive the task as "baby work" (Slavin 1986). One disadvantage of cross-age tutoring, however, is that it is not as easy to manage as regular peer tutoring, because it requires at least two teachers to organize the activity.

Another possibility for setting up tutoring programs is to include parents or other adult community members as volunteer tutors; this can lead to increased community involvement, and it promotes reading as more than simply a school-related activity.

Assessment:
Purposes and Approaches

Assessment of student learning can serve many purposes, and an understanding of these purposes can help teachers choose an appropriate assessment approach. For example, when evaluation includes the assignment of grades, teachers have a convenient vehicle for reporting student performance and progress to students, parents, and others. When a teacher provides comments and corrections, students receive valuable feedback that can improve future efforts. Additional purposes for reading assessment include:

1) *Highlighting assessment as a meaning-making process.* Approaches that serve this purpose put a premium on engaging students in their reading materials and encouraging creativity, personal response, and interpretation. They have potential to promote better learning and a more in-depth understanding of subject matter.

2) *Providing teachers with diagnostic information on student reading level.* Approaches that serve this purpose might be used to inform the instruction of students who have particular reading problems. Once a student's strengths and weaknesses have been identified, the instructor can determine which strategies might address the weaknesses.

APPROACHES THAT HIGHLIGHT ASSESSMENT AS A MEANING-MAKING PROCESS

Book reports, quizzes, and short-answer tests are some of the more traditional ways that a secondary school teacher might assess student understanding of assigned reading. These types of evaluation have come under criticism in recent years, however, because they fail to allow the reader to *create meaning* and *respond* to the text. Rather, they encourage the reader to passively recite or recall a reading's facts and details—which is likely to lose the interest and motivation of the typical adolescent reader.

As reading has come to be viewed as an interactive process that involves a transaction between reader and text, parallel evaluation methods have been developed. One example is portfolio assessment, in which students create portfolios of written work that include items such as their personal responses to reading assignments. The rationale behind these new types of assessment is that because reading is a dynamic process, it requires a dynamic form of assessment.

This is not to say that quizzes and standardized tests are without value altogether. There are certainly instances when a quiz can be useful, such as when a teacher needs a quick method of determining how much students have understood from a story. However, if used as the exclusive form of assessment, quizzes can have detrimental effects on learners. Because this form of assessment usually emphasizes recall of the plot itself and does not encourage students to engage in a more substantive analysis of a story, students trained in the "quiz habit" are likely to experience difficulty in subsequent writing assignments that call for in-depth interpretation (Johannessen 1994). This argument is supported by a case study of an English teacher who found that putting less emphasis on summaries of literature—coupled with the introduction of dialogue journals—resulted in the expression of more substantive ideas about literature, as seen in classroom discussion as well as in the student journals. The author of the study notes that "less emphasis on summary encouraged deeper analysis of reactions to specific characters and incidents, the very exploration of which necessitated incorporating the facts [the teacher] sought as reassurance that they had understood" (Gross 1992, 11).

In addition, a review of the research on classroom evaluation indicates that dynamic types of assessment tend to promote better learning. The author concludes that classroom evaluation all too often emphasizes the importance of isolated pieces of information, when in fact information is remembered better and is often more useful when it is learned within a broader framework of meaningful interrelationships (Crooks 1988).

Two basic goals of dynamic reading instruction are heightening student engagement and instilling in students a love of reading. However, these goals may appear to be incompatible with an approach that always holds students accountable for what they read. One possible remedy for this dilemma is to provide time for assessment-free independent reading during the school day (see page 21). This is not to suggest that assessment should be eliminated entirely; rather, the trick is to find ways to turn the assessment process itself into something that excites students about reading, encourages them to develop their own understandings of a text, and provides information that can be used to improve the instructional process.

The new emphasis on assessment as a meaning-making process stands in sharp contrast to the traditional definition of assessment as something produced *after* the learning has occurred, in order to measure what has been learned. In fact, assessment should be part of the learning process, not separate from it. Learning can occur *while* students are creating something that will be assessed, as well as once they receive teacher feedback on the product they have created.

Although assessment methods that emphasize student meaning-making— such as essay writing, portfolios, and personal anthologies—may seem more relevant for English classes than for content-area classes, most can be easily adapted for content-area assignments. For example, portfolios are now being used more and more in math classes; these portfolios might include student-formulated problems or samples of journal writing related to mathematical concepts being studied (Crowley 1993).

Teachers who implement these methods will need to be aware that they may have to spend more time evaluating and providing feedback on student work. It will probably take longer to grade a personal response essay than a short-answer test about the plot of a story. At the same time, learners will need to increase their time investment as well, as they are called upon to make more thoughtful interpretations and responses to a text.

ESSAYS

Essay writing is an integral part of assessment in the English classroom, and is frequently used in the content-area classroom as well. Findings of a national study of high school literature programs underscore the value of essay writing as a learning tool. This study found that English teachers in award-winning schools placed more emphasis on essays than did those in other schools (Applebee 1993).

The nature of essay assignments can vary widely. An essay assignment might call for formal analysis of a text only, or it might also call upon the reader to include a personal response. The national study mentioned above found that text-based essays are assigned far more often than essays that stress a reader's personal response or interpretation (Applebee 1993). Personal response-oriented essays have been found to be comparable to text-based essays in their effects on the understanding of literary texts, however, even when students are more familiar with a formal essay approach (Marshall 1987). In Marshall's study, personal response-oriented essay assignments asked students to explain and elaborate upon their responses to a story, drawing on their own values and experiences to make sense of their reactions to the text.

When the researchers interviewed these students, they found that they sometimes perceived formal analytic writing as merely "an exercise in fulfilling their teacher's expectations rather than an occasion for thinking through the literature," while personal essays provided an opportunity to begin the process of independent analysis.

PORTFOLIOS

A portfolio is a collection of formal and informal student work, connected to what has been read and studied, that reveals student progress. Portfolio items range from self-assessments to teacher observations, attitude and interest surveys, writing samples (both complete and in-progress), evidence that the student reads for enjoyment and information, retellings, summaries, responses to readings, and journal entries. Portfolios have been criticized for not providing measures of overall student progress similar to those provided by large-scale assessments, as well as for low interrater reliability (the consistency with which different readers assign the same score to a single portfolio). However, portfolios do show promise as tools for assessing individual student progress and for encouraging teachers to change their instructional approaches in the direction of more active student involvement (Viadero 1995).

Portfolios encourage student involvement in two important ways: First, they call on each student to document and reflect upon his or her own progress. Second, while students compile portfolios, they decide which works to include and why. This process of selection—again, with the help of teacher modeling—can foster the development of personal criteria against which a student can judge quality and effort, thereby encouraging future efforts to improve.

PERSONAL ANTHOLOGIES

Developing a personal anthology can motivate learners to read widely and to make connections between the different works they read. The advantage of this assignment is that while it calls upon students to create a finished product for evaluation, it highlights the reading activity itself as something that is enjoyable and personally meaningful. Students create a personal anthology by acting as editor: they search for works of literature that best connect with their interests and tastes, develop a theme, and then compile these works into an anthology (Sullivan 1988).

Sullivan advises teachers to instruct students that, as they compile their personal anthology, they should read only works that interest them, and put away anything that they find boring. The theme of a personal anthology should be entirely student-selected, so that students may focus on those interests or ideas that have greatest personal meaning to them. Sullivan writes, "The connection with self explains the almost fierce sense of pride and ownership that my students feel about their anthologies" (28). Anthologies developed by students could also form the basis for future work or reading by other students. The product of assessment can thus be applied to different purposes.

Although students are allowed a great deal of choice, the teacher should be precise about certain requirements. For example, directions should be given about general types of literature to be read. The teacher might require specific numbers of poems, essays, and works of short fiction—all divided among different genres, such as science fiction, works by Southern writers, and works by fellow students. Teachers should also develop stringent guidelines as to the actual preparation of the anthology. Sullivan recommends requiring elements such as a title page, a table of contents, a preface with opinions about the works chosen and why they were chosen, and a bibliography. The anthology could be evaluated by assigning each element a maximum number of points, and adding the points in each category to arrive at a total score.

OTHER ALTERNATIVE EVALUATION METHODS

A number of other ideas are listed below. These are all appropriate for language arts assessment (that is, when evaluating students' understanding of a story), and could also be applied in the content areas, such as when studying historically significant events or people relating to that particular subject area.

- *Continuation of a story.* Have students continue the plot after the end of the story, by describing what happens to the main character.

- *Point of view.* Have students rewrite the material from the point of view of another character who was not a narrator.

- *Rewrite the ending.* Students often have their own ideas about how a story, either fiction or nonfiction, should have ended. Rewriting can be done individually or by groups creating scripts; the scripts can then be acted out for the rest of the class.

- *Newspapers.* Students can write newspaper articles about an event or several events in the text or historical occurrence. These can be interviews, feature articles, or photo essays.

- *Literary panel.* Students can play the roles of characters from a story or historical event. They form a panel and are interviewed about the parts they play.

- *Relating material to themselves.* For example, if a class reads *Huckleberry Finn*, students could write a modern-day version of the novel, casting themselves as Huck, describing their journeys and struggles. Alternatively, if a science class were reading about efforts to develop a polio vaccine, they might compare this to how they feel about the efforts to find a cure for a modern-day illness.

- *Paradigms.* A paradigm can be a graphic display on posterboard, in which students relate their hobbies and interests to the elements of the written material. For example, one student diagrammed the opposing themes of depression and resurrection in *The Grapes of Wrath* across a basketball court; another illustrated and explained the novel's rising and falling action by depicting a surfer approaching waves (Guzzetti 1990).

- *Scripting a meeting of characters.* Students can be asked to imagine that four of the characters from the materials they have read have gathered in one place. Working in small groups, they imagine what would happen and create a script. They perform the script in front of classmates, and then write reflective essays on their experience working on this project (Tuley 1994).

- Other methods of evaluation include creating drawings of the main characters, rewriting the text as a play or poem, and developing book covers, collages, and games.

Student projects should be evaluated on the basis of how consistent they are with the material presented, and on whether they have considered relevant concepts, issues, and events. Naturally, some forms of evaluation will work better with some material than others. For example, a story or historical event with a controversial ending would be particularly appropriate for an assignment to rewrite the ending.

APPROACHES DESIGNED TO PROVIDE TEACHERS WITH INFORMATION ON STUDENT READING LEVEL

When working with students whose reading deficiencies significantly interfere with their attention to the material, teachers may need to use specific techniques to assess the nature of the problems. Gathering information on student reading level allows educators to identify students' specific strengths and weaknesses in terms of reading comprehension abilities, to identify teaching strategies that target the weak areas, and to decide what kinds of reading strategies students need to practice. Several methods of gathering information are discussed below: teacher observation, the cloze procedure, retellings, miscue analysis, and informal reading inventories.

Many of these methods are typically used by reading specialists, and are used less often by content-area teachers and English teachers; for example, most reading specialists have received special training in the technique of miscue analysis. Other techniques, such as teacher observation and retellings, are more familiar to teachers. The purpose of this section is to provide an overview of some different diagnostic tools, in order to inform teachers of the kinds of steps that might be taken with students who have reading difficulties—even if the teachers will not actually be implementing the diagnosis. Some of these tools also could be used by subject-area teachers, perhaps in collaboration with the reading specialist. When teachers do not have reading specialists available, they will need additional administrative support for their own efforts to learn about and use diagnostic tools.

Gathering this kind of diagnostic information can be an important tool for teachers, providing information on reading level and reading progress that can help to inform instruction, as well as subsequent graded assessment and other feedback that teachers give students about their performance. Diagnostic tools need not be used with all students all the time. They are often most effectively employed when a teacher is concerned about a particular student who is having difficulty with the information presented in the written materials.

TEACHER OBSERVATION

Perhaps the most reliable and useful information about reading level can be gained by the observations teachers make on a day-to-day basis. These observations can provide a more accurate and complete picture than the snapshot provided by a reading test. Teachers might record their observations about individual students, either in a notebook or on a form or checklist. Because of the time required for tracking all students with notebook comments, teachers may choose instead to write about the progress of just a few students who are especially in need of assistance.

Teachers might also record their observations on a form that gives space for brief comments about each student, or check off skills and behaviors from a checklist. These tools are designed to record general reading skills or specific behaviors such as comprehension, motivation and interest, and vocabulary usage. Because the space for recording is small, it encourages brief comments that do not require a great deal of time.

CLOZE PROCEDURE

This is a useful, time-efficient procedure for determining reading level, and it also can be used for assessing the readability of classroom reading material. The Cloze procedure requires several steps (Cheek 1992):

1) Select a passage of approximately 300 words.

2) Use a formula to determine readability (see pages 71-72).

3) Retype the passage leaving the first and last sentence intact, but delete every fifth word.

4) Type an underline to replace the omitted word (all underlines should be of the same length).

5) Instruct students to fill in the blanks with the words that best complete the sentences.

6) Score student responses, counting only exact matches as correct. Criteria: 58-100 percent correct is independent reading level, 44 percent to 57 percent correct is instructional reading level, and 0 percent to 43 percent correct is frustration reading level.

RETELLINGS

The retelling technique involves giving students time to read a passage, perhaps also allowing for time to take notes or to rehearse information, and then asking them to write a retelling without referring to the original passage. This technique gives the teacher insight into student comprehension processes, such as *how* information is organized into a whole and *how much* information is gained from the passage.

MISCUE ANALYSIS

This technique, developed from the research of Kenneth and Yetta Goodman, involves examining the oral reading performance of learners. The word *miscue* refers to an instance when the reader reads something that is different from the printed text. This approach does not involve an exact scoring of reading level, but rather a qualitative analysis of the reader's strengths and weaknesses, based on the student's oral reading of a passage and retelling of it. For more information on miscue analysis, see Goodman, Watson, and Burke (1987).

INFORMAL READING INVENTORIES (IRIS)

Informal reading inventories are often constructed by the teacher or the reading specialist (they are also sometimes found in basals). The benefit of a teacher-constructed IRI is that it is tailored to the materials in the specific instructional program, because it typically uses a sampling of curriculum materials. Also, teachers can devise an IRI that will highlight the constructive nature of reading, as evidenced by the following example.

Brozo (1990) developed an IRI that emphasizes that a student's ability to comprehend is not fixed or constant, but varies across tasks and settings and is influenced by a variety of factors, such as prior knowledge and interest. Components include:

1) *Diagnostic interview:* Teacher first collects information about students' reading attitudes and reading interests, what kind of reading strategies they use, any background information they have about the topic, and their awareness of the goals and purposes of reading.

2) *Preparing to read:* Teacher builds motivation for reading the passage by activating background knowledge, setting purposes for reading, and preteaching important vocabulary and concepts.

3) *Reading silently:* This allows students to work through miscues on their own and to identify unknown words before reading out loud.

4) *During oral reading:* At this time, the teacher should model comprehension processes with self-questioning and by thinking out loud. Students give self-reports on their own comprehension strategies.

5) *After reading.* Students generate retellings. The teacher can extend student understanding of the passage with activities that connect their prior knowledge with the newly learned content.

Issues Specific to
Content-Area Reading Instruction

Many issues, ideas, and suggestions that were described earlier are relevant to (and in some cases, *critical* for) content-area reading instruction. This section, however, focuses on issues that are specific to content reading. First, three of the core content areas (social studies, science, and math) are examined individually in terms of the special reading skills they demand and the techniques that might develop these skills. Next, approaches for using literature in content-area classrooms are described. Another concern that is addressed is textbook usage, and ways in which content teachers might use textbooks most effectively.

READING SKILLS NEEDED
IN SOME SPECIFIC CONTENT AREAS

There is great variety among the content areas in terms of demands placed on the reader. It stands to reason, for example, that the reading skills needed in math class differ sharply from those required for reading in social studies. The focus here is on three of the core content areas—mathematics, science, and social studies—as examples of how reading skills and reading instruction can be integrated into content areas. In addition to helping students achieve greater mastery in the specific content area discussed, many of the reading skills can also be applied to other situations.

READING IN SOCIAL STUDIES

Social studies demands not only basic skills such as recall of details, sequence of events, and recognition of main ideas, but also a higher level of critical thinking involving interpretation, synthesis, and analysis. Cochran writes that the challenge to social studies students is to master facts, and then "think about how these facts contributed to the events of the past as well as how they can be used to predict future events" (1993, 3). Two important critical reading skills are recognizing cause-and-effect relationships and distinguishing fact from opinion.

Teachers can help students recognize cause-and-effect relationships by:

- *Presenting real-life examples.*

- *Calling attention to signal words in expository writing.* Signal words include "because," "therefore," "so," and "in order to." Have students find examples of these words in their textbook.

- *Elaborating on cause-and-effect situations during the school day.* For example, ask students: "What would happen if you didn't turn in your home-work? Why would that happen?" (Hickey 1990).

Some techniques teachers can use to assist students in developing the ability to distinguish fact from opinion include:

- Asking students to analyze newspaper articles, examine the statements presented in them, and determine which ones are verifiable facts.

- Having students restate factual information as opinion, and opinion as fact.

- Dividing the class into pairs, with each pair given a list of names, events, and terminology related to a current social studies topic. One partner compiles a list of facts related to the topic, while the other collects opinions. Students then work in groups of four, where each pair takes turns reading one of its statements and asking the other pair whether the statement is fact or opinion (Hickey 1990).

Other crucial skills in social studies reading include identifying propaganda techniques, identifying the author's purpose (including obvious public purposes and possible "hidden" purposes), and recognizing bias and emotionally charged words. In order to motivate students to develop some of these skills, a teacher could provide students with two or more accounts of an historical event, or even newspaper accounts of a current event. Students would then be asked to compare and contrast the authors' points of view, accuracy, and use of bias or persuasive language.

READING IN SCIENCE

Science reading materials are often particularly challenging for students with reading difficulties. This is because these materials are typically characterized by an expository style, terse and exact wording, and an abundance of technical vocabulary, symbols, and formulas. However, comprehension of scientific materials can be enhanced by using many of the techniques mentioned previously, such as metacognitive strategies, cooperative learning groups, vocabulary development methods, and supplementing the textbook with materials such as scientific articles in popular magazines or profiles of famous scientists. Science teachers also can make use of analogies in order to help students make connections between the abstract concepts they read about and their previous experience. Another technique that promotes greater conceptual understanding is asking students to make predictions and discuss ideas when they are just beginning to learn about a scientific concept.

Science involves tasks such as finding solutions to problems, gathering data, conducting experiments, and interpreting results. For this reason, science teachers should emphasize such reading skills as following directions and drawing conclusions. Also essential are problem-solving skills: defining the problem, looking at it thoroughly, and then organizing a plan of attack for solving it. Moreover, science teachers should encourage students to be risk takers when they read, considering more than one possible solution to a problem (Cochran 1993).

"Science anxiety" is a term that has spawned a great deal of discussion in recent years. Educators are concerned about many students' low level of success in science, and their avoidance of studying it whenever possible (Mallow 1991). Many students perceive science as a field suited for only the most intellectual, a field that is too difficult for them to understand. A legitimate goal for science teachers, then, should be to raise students' awareness of science as an approach for investigating everyday problems, as well as those beyond our comprehension (Cochran 1993). By using articles about scientific current events or materials about people who have chosen a career in science, science teachers may help students see the applicability of science to real life, as well as broadening the types of science reading materials available for use in the classroom.

Teachers can support learning of science vocabulary and concepts in several ways. Hands-on science activities such as conducting experiments and gathering data provide teachers with an opportunity to use content-area vocabulary words in a relevant context. This approach will help students to understand vocabulary words more deeply. For example, learning the meaning of the word *permeable* is easier and more meaningful if the word is used in the context of a relevant lab experiment (Barton 1997).

READING IN MATHEMATICS

Math texts are like science texts in that they include many symbols and are written compactly. Yet, math texts are unique reading materials in several important ways. For example, they include a large amount of nonverbal material and therefore require slow and deliberate reading for comprehension. In addition, mathematicians take common words and add technical definitions to them— such as the word *and*, which usually means *plus* when used in math problems. Another unique aspect of mathematical reading is that, in the case of equations, each number or symbol and its position on the page relative to others is especially important. In the case of word problems, the order of the words, as well as the functional relation between words, are crucial to the text's meaning. Word problems are made more challenging by the fact that different components are linked together by prepositions; students reading these problems may need special instruction in preposition usage. Also, the students reading these problems often are not aware that analytical reading is necessary, and they may lack experience and skill in this kind of reading (MacGregor 1990).

Strategies for teaching reading in math include:

- When presenting students with word problems, ask them for definitions of key terms and interpretations of important phrases.

- Ask students to rephrase a complicated word problem in their own words, perhaps breaking the problem down into a series of simple sentences (Nolan 1984).

- Provide direct instruction in reading math textbooks in terms of four factors: terminology (identifying and learning only the terms needed for the problem on which the student is working), eye patterns (reading math expressions involving parentheses from the inside and moving outward), graph/text interaction (stopping at intermediate stages of a sample problem to identify patterns emerging on a graph), and reading direction (sometimes starting from the final step of the solution rather than reading problems from top to bottom) (Ostler 1997).

- Use the chalkboard and the overhead projector to help students with their reading. As teachers visually represent the material, a discussion of mathematical symbols and terms will occur (Cochran 1993).

- Model and allow students to practice translating mathematical word sentences to symbols, and equations to words; the translation can be written directly underneath the original expression to illustrate the correspondence (Fuentes 1998).

- Use the technique of thinking out loud in order to model how one might interpret a problem and go about solving it.

- Increase interest and motivation for reading mathematical language by encouraging recreational reading of materials with high math content, such as earned run averages in baseball and statistical information from surveys (Fuentes 1998).

- Ask students to keep a math journal, writing out definitions or exploring concepts.

- Implement post-reading discussions in math class about topics such as: new or familiar ideas in the reading, real-world applications that the concepts might have, and the steps that the author recommended following versus the steps that students actually used (Tanner and Casados 1998).

To reinforce what was stated earlier, many of the approaches mentioned above—while especially helpful for improving learning in a particular content area—provide the student with reading-related skills generalizable to other settings. For example, an understanding of cause-and-effect relationships discussed in the section on social studies is not only important in social studies, but is also essential in the fields of mathematics and science, as well as in everyday life.

USING LITERATURE IN THE CONTENT-AREA CLASSROOM

High-quality literature is not the exclusive domain of English classes: when integrated into other content-area courses, it can more fully develop ideas and concepts than a textbook alone. Many high-quality picture books are appealing to all age groups and offer a wealth of information. For example, the *Eyewitness Readers* series explains abstract concepts in science and math through models and diagrams. Narrative picture books such as David Macauley's *Cathedral* and Maruki's *Hiroshima No Pika* provide rich detail on historical sites or events (Vacca and Vacca 1993).

In their book *Content Area Reading*, Vacca and Vacca (1993) write:

> Fiction entices readers to interact with texts from a number of perspectives that are impossible to achieve in nonfiction alone. Fantasy, traditional (e.g., folktales and myths), historical, and realistic fiction, for example, help readers to step outside of their actual worlds for a while to consider a subject from a different point of view. And by doing so, they learn something about what it means to be a human being on this planet of ours (p. 301).

Because of the variety of topics found in trade books for adolescent readers, they lend themselves to interdisciplinary connections. Pottle (1996) offers the following guidelines for finding trade books that provide the strongest across-the-curriculum connections:

1) Are the book's characters believable? That is, do they act and react as real people do?

2) Do the characters change during the course of the book?

3) By reading this book, will students learn more about a scientific concept and its practical application?

4) Are the statements that are presented as facts accurate?

5) Is the novel set in a specific time period? Is this time period represented realistically?

6) Has the book been prepared with care? Is the illustration on the cover eye-catching? Is the print clear and easily read? If there are illustrations, do they enhance the text?

❖ USING TEXTBOOKS ❖

Textbooks are often the mainstay of content-area classrooms. Most material is presented through the textbook, and lectures and tests are structured around it. Studies report that students spend as much as 75 percent of classroom time and 90 percent of homework time involved with textbook material (Ciborowski 1992).

Although they remain the central learning tool in content-area classrooms, textbooks have been the focus of substantial debate in recent years. They have been criticized for stilted writing, covering too much information in too little depth, avoiding controversy, and poor instructional design (Ciborowski 1992).

Ciborowski (1992) contends that good textbooks meet four broad criteria:

1) They include pre-reading strategies that connect learning to student experience, thereby igniting student interest.

2) They emphasize the importance of teaching comprehension and thinking skills as well as content.

3) They describe novel assessment practices that will give teachers ideas for helping students consolidate new textbook knowledge with existing knowledge.

4) They are written in a style that is both engaging and well-organized.

However, even textbooks that meet these criteria can be too difficult for some students whose reading skills are far below grade level.

READABILITY AND READABILITY FORMULAS

Educators determine the readability level of a textbook for two purposes:

1) Individual teachers might have the opportunity to assist with textbook selection.

2) Once the textbook is in use, teachers want to determine whether certain parts of it (or the entire book) are appropriate for the reading level of their students.

What teachers learn about the readability level of the textbook will guide decisions about adapting the material for their students.

A variety of *readability formulas* exist. Their purpose is twofold: to help publishers develop texts that are at the reading level for which they were intended; and to help educators determine the reading level of instructional materials. Most readability formulas are based on average sentence length and complexity of words within several sample passages from a text. For example, one widely used formula, the Fry Readability Graph, requires the random selection of three passages within a text. By counting out 100 words and then counting the number of sentences and syllables within the 100 words, an average sentence length and average number of syllables can be obtained. These numbers are then plotted on a graph designed for estimating readability, and the area in which the plotted point falls gives the approximate grade level. Other readability formulas include the Flesch Reading Ease Formula, the McLaughlin SMOG Index, and the Dale-Chall Formula. Readability can also be determined with a cloze procedure, which involves replacing every fifth or tenth word with a blank after the first paragraph in unfamiliar text, until about 50 blanks have been inserted. The text should be drawn from the beginning of an unfamiliar chapter in the content textbook. If students fill in 35 to 45 percent of the words correctly (not counting synonyms), the text is at an appropriate level (Manning 1999).

While readability formulas can provide valuable information about a text, they do not consider some of the most important student factors that determine readability, such as prior knowledge and motivation. In addition, they do not take into account text features such as text clarity, chapter titles, paragraph divisions, subtitles, and illustrations—all of which can improve readability.

One alternate technique that does take the above factors into account is the FLIP framework (Schumm and Mangrum 1991). This technique calls upon the students to evaluate the difficulty of reading material. It is grounded in the principle that readers first need to have an idea of the difficulty of a task before they can plan how to approach it.

FLIP stands for Friendliness, Language, Interest, and Prior knowledge; students are asked to flip through the text and look for those four factors. Specifically, the factors call upon students to evaluate the text in the following ways:

- *Friendliness*: Does the assignment contain "friendly elements" such as a table of contents, headings, and a glossary?

- *Language*: How difficult is the language? (What is the vocabulary level; how complicated are the sentences?)

- *Interest*: How interesting is my reading assignment? (Look at the title, introduction, headings, summary, pictures, and graphics, and rate how interesting or boring the assignment is based on these factors.)

- *Prior knowledge*: What do I already know about the topic?

Students add the ratings they give each of the four elements and determine whether the level of the assignment is "comfortable," "somewhat comfortable," or "uncomfortable." They then complete a follow-up survey in which they determine an appropriate reading rate and budget their reading or study time. Students using the FLIP framework were found to make more realistic predictions about estimated reading/study time and to improve their test performance.

ADAPTING TEXTBOOKS THAT ARE IN USE

Once the reading level of a text is approximated, the text may require adaptation to accommodate various reading levels. Adaptation becomes even more crucial in the upper grades, for two reasons: multilevel texts for content-area courses are available less often and students in the upper grades vary more than younger students in terms of their reading levels. Research suggests that the reading ability range within an age group is equal to two-thirds of the chrono-logical age. For example, while students in a fourth-grade class might be as much as three grade levels lower or higher than average fourth-grade reading level, students in a tenth-grade class might be as much as *five* grade levels lower or higher than the average tenth-grade reading level. This increased range in reading ability in the upper grades accentuates the importance of adapting a textbook when it is too hard for some students to read. Furthermore, adapting a textbook by supplementing it with diverse sources of information, including movies and works of literature, will enhance student interest.

According to one study (Schumm et al. 1992), middle and high school students did not feel that they were being exposed to the kinds of instructional adaptations that would help them understand the textbook. These students endorsed the following suggestions for dealing with a textbook that is hard to understand:

- *Rewrite content material.* This can be done either by teachers or students. Teachers can tailor difficult material to the reading level of students; students who understand the text can rewrite it for peers who do not understand.

- *Supplement textbooks with other textbooks written at a lower level.* Some textbooks are published in multilevel versions. That is, two different versions of a textbook may appear the same and may cover the same material page for page, but the material within the books differs in terms of readability level.

- *Supplement textbooks with trade books.* This exposes students to a number of different kinds of contact with concepts and enhances comprehension.

- *Create in-class vertical files.* These are teacher-created (or student-created) files of materials, such as magazine or newspaper articles, relating to specific topics. Up-to-date information makes students aware of the relevance of the subject to their own lives.

- *Use audiovisual aids.* These might include films, audiotapes, television, and pictures.

One caution: those who rewrite textbooks (either publishers who are trying to attain a certain readability score or teachers who want to make difficult material more understandable for their students) run the risk of oversimplifying concepts and taking out important words in their efforts to shorten texts. When sentences are shortened to conform to readability formulas, important words such as *however, because,* and *in addition to* may be deleted, and the writing then becomes stilted, dull, and less coherent (Ciborowski 1992). A study of eighth-grade readers demonstrates that both less-able readers and able readers gain more vocabulary knowledge from reading an *elaborated* text than from reading a simpler, revised text (Herman et al. 1987). The authors note: "Texts will not necessarily be made easier by making them short and superficial. What is critical is that they convey important information precisely, with interconnections fully explained at a level of specificity appropriate for readers who do not know much about the subject matter" (281).

INSERVICE ON USING TEXTBOOKS EFFECTIVELY

A study by Davey (1988) about teacher use of textbooks indicates that content-area teachers might profit from inservice activities that focus on flexible textbook adjustments. Davey targets five specific areas as topics for inservice programs:

1) grouping strategies for cooperative learning from textbooks;

2) overviews of text selections prior to assignments;

3) using a variety of information sources;

4) ample vocabulary development before and after reading textbooks;

5) specific good reading strategies, such as self-questioning and summarizing.

Conclusion

R eading is not simply an isolated subject that is mastered in elementary
school and then need never be taught again. On the contrary, reading—and
literacy in general—is a critical tool that must continue to be developed in
adolescence and beyond. Our reading abilities are fundamentally tied to other
important life skills, such as communicating thoughts through writing, discussing and analyzing information with others, gaining knowledge, improving
vocabulary, and following written directions. Furthermore, reading for pleasure
is often an end in itself. Getting absorbed in good books allows individuals to
develop their personal interests, take time out from hectic activities, and engage
in a creative solitary activity—which can contribute to a greater sense of balance
amid life's pastimes and pursuits.

In many ways, adolescence is an opportune time to enhance reading and
thinking skills. Middle and high school students are at a stage in life in which
they are developing cognitive abilities that allow them to grapple with more
complex ideas. They are also dealing with important issues involving identity,
relations with others, and planning for their futures as adults. Educators can take
advantage of these unique circumstances when developing reading instruction.
For example, they can both challenge and strengthen students' emerging think-

ing abilities by using techniques such as student debates, thematic units, and small-group discussion.

In order to successfully develop reading skills, readers must be active. Active readers are engaged with the text; they search for meaning; they are aware of their purposes for reading; they are interested in what they are learning; and they connect what they are reading with their prior knowledge or their own personal experiences. Research findings underscore the importance of promoting active reading. Some elements of instruction that have been found to be effective include: small-group discussions about reading materials, activating background knowledge before reading, instruction in metacognitive strategies such as monitoring comprehension, opportunities to respond to reading by writing in dialogue journals, interactive types of computer-assisted reading activities, and choice in reading materials.

A number of studies have found interactive approaches to be highly benefi- cial for low-achieving secondary students. At the same time, though, these and other students need support to develop component skills in order to become independent readers. Research findings in this area are encouraging, indicating that strategic reading skills can be taught, and that textbook adaptations are effective in increasing understanding of the material.

The issue of assessment must be carefully considered. The recent literature on assessment has emphasized the importance of matching the test to the task: if reading is an active process, assessment of reading comprehension should also be active. Whereas short-answer and standardized tests have a place in the curricu- lum, more emphasis should be placed on forms of assessment that promote learning as a meaning-making process. Assessment should be treated as a *part* of the learning process, not as an entirely separate process.

A number of suggestions have been provided to secondary school educators, both English teachers and other content-area teachers, for integrating reading instruction into the curriculum. When reading instruction and reading-related activities are incorporated into the curriculum, rather than simply appended to it, the goal of improving reading skills becomes time-efficient. Moreover, this approach has the potential to draw attention to reading as a meaningful and enjoyable activity, and it serves as a demonstration of the central role that literacy plays in the many and varied tasks of our lives.

References

Allington, Richard L. and Anne McGill-Franzen. 1990. "Children with Reading Problems: How We Wrongfully Classify Them and Fail to Teach Many to Read." In *Early Reading Difficulties: Their Misclassification and Treatment as Learning Disabilities (ERS Research Digest)*, pp. 4-10. Arlington, VA: Educational Research Service.

Anderson, Margaret A., Nona A. Tollefson, and Edwyna C. Gilbert. 1985. "Giftedness and Reading: A Cross-Sectional View of Differences in Reading Attitudes and Behaviors." *Gifted Child Quarterly* Vol. 29, No. 1: 186-189.

Applebee, Arthur N. 1993. *Literature in the Secondary School: Studies of Curriculum and Instruction in the United States*. Urbana, Illinois: National Council of Teachers of English.

Atwell, Nancie. 1987. *In the Middle: Writing, Reading, and Learning with Adolescents*. Portsmouth, NH: Heinemann.

Baldwin, R. Scott, Ziva Peleg-Bruckner, and Ann H. McClintock. 1985. "Effects of Topic Interest and Prior Knowledge on Reading." *Reading Research Quarterly* Vol. 20, No. 4: 497-504.

Beentjes, Johannes W.J. and Tom H.A. Van der Voort. 1988. "Television's Impact on Children's Reading Skills: A Review of Research." *Reading Research Quarterly* Vol. 23, No. 4: 389-413.

Belloni, Loretta Frances and Eugene A. Jongsma. 1978. "The Effects of Interest on Reading Comprehension of Low-Achieving Students." *Journal of Reading* Vol. 22, No. 2: 106-109.

Bernhardt, Bill. 1994. "Reading and Writing Between the Lines: An Interactive Approach Using Computers." *Journal of Reading* Vol. 37, No. 6: 458-463.

Birnbaum, June Cannell. 1986. "Reflective Thought: The Connection Between Reading and Writing." In *Convergences: Transactions in Reading and Writing*. Ed. Bruce T. Petersen, pp. 30-45. Urbana, IL: National Council of Teachers of English.

Blanchard, Jay. 1989. "An Exploratory Inquiry: The Milieu of Research in Secondary, Content-Area Reading Methodology Textbooks." *Teacher Education Quarterly* Vol. 16, No. 1: 51-63.

Bonds, Charles W., Lella Gant Bonds, and Walter Peach. 1992. "Metacognition: Developing Independence in Learning." *The Clearing House* Vol. 66, No. 1: 56-59.

Brozo, William G. 1990. "Learning How At-Risk Readers Learn Best: A Case for Interactive Assessment." *Journal of Reading* Vol. 33, No. 7: 522-527.

Burroughs, Robert. 1993. "Supporting Successful Literature Programs: Lessons From a New National Survey." *School Library Media Quarterly* Vol. 21, No. 3: 159-163.

Call, Patricia E. 1991. "SQ3R + What I Know Sheet = One Strong Strategy (Open to Suggestion)." *Journal of Reading* Vol. 35, No. 1: 50-52.

Carbo, Marie. 1987. "Deprogramming Reading Failure: Giving Unequal Learners an Equal Chance." *Phi Delta Kappan* Vol. 69, No. 3: 197-201.

Carbo, Marie. 1994. "Sharply Increasing the Reading Ability of Potential Dropouts." In *Using What We Know About At-Risk Youth: Lessons from the Field*. Ed. Robert C. Morris, pp. 129-138. Lancaster, PA: Technomic Publishing Co., Inc.

Carlsen, G. Robert and Anne Sherrill. 1988. *Voices of Readers: How We Come to Love Books*. Urbana, IL: National Council of Teachers of English.

Chall, Jeanne S. and Mary E. Curtis. 1992. "Teaching the Disabled or Below-Average Reader." In *What Research Has to Say About Reading Instruction*. Second edition. Ed. S. Jay Samuels and Alan E. Farstrup, pp. 253-276. Newark, DE: International Reading Association.

Chan, Lorna K.S. 1994. "Relationship of Motivation, Strategic Learning, and Reading Achievement in Grades 5, 7, and 9." *Journal of Experimental Education* Vol. 62, No. 4: 319-339.

Cheek, Earl H., Jr. 1992. "Selecting Appropriate Informal Reading Assessment Procedures." *Middle School Journal* Vol. 24, No. 1: 33-36.

Ciborowski, Jean. 1992. *Textbooks and the Students Who Can't Read Them: A Guide to Teaching Content*. Boston, MA: Brookline Books.

Cochran, Judith A. 1993. *Reading in the Content Areas for Junior High and High School*. Boston, MA: Allyn and Bacon.

Crooks, Terence J. 1988. "The Impact of Classroom Evaluation Practices on Students." *Review of Educational Research* Vol. 58, No. 4: 438-481.

Crowley, Mary L. 1993. "Student Mathematics Portfolio: More Than a Display Case." *The Mathematics Teacher* Vol. 86, No. 7: 544-547.

Davey, Beth. 1988. "How Do Classroom Teachers Use Their Textbooks?" *Journal of Reading* Vol. 31, No. 4: 340-345.

Davidson, Judith and David Koppenhaver. 1993. *Adolescent Literacy: What Works and Why*. New York: Garland Publishing, Inc.

DeGroff, Linda. 1990. "Is There a Place for Computers in Whole Language Classrooms?" *The Reading Teacher* Vol. 33, No. 7: 568-572.

Dillner, Martha. 1994. "Using Hypermedia to Enhance Content Area Instruction." *Journal of Reading* Vol. 37, No. 4: 260-270.

Divine, Katherine P. and Richard E. Whanger. 1990. "Use of a Computer Learning Laboratory With At-Risk High School Students." *Educational Technology* Vol. 30, No. 6: 46-48.

Ecroyd, Catherine Ann. 1991. "Motivating Students Through Reading Aloud." *English Journal* Vol. 80, No. 6: 76-78.

Eeds, Maryann and Deborah Wells. 1989. "Grand Conversations: An Exploration of Meaning Construction in Literature Study Groups." *Research in the Teaching of English* Vol. 23, No. 1: 4-29.

Fuhler, Carol J. 1994. "Response Journals: Just One More Time With Feeling." *Journal of Reading* Vol. 37, No. 5: 400-405.

Garner, Ruth and Victoria Chou Hare. 1984. "Efficacy of Text Lookback Training for Poor Comprehenders at Two Age Levels." *Journal of Educational Research* Vol. 77, No. 6: 376-381.

Gauthier, Lane Roy. 1989. "Understanding Content Material (In the Classroom)." *Reading Teacher* Vol. 43, No. 3: 266-267.

Gee, Thomas C. and Nora Forester. 1988. "Moving Reading Instruction Beyond the Reading Classroom." *Journal of Reading* Vol. 31, No. 6: 505-511.

Gentile, Lance M. and Merna M. McMillan. 1994. "Critical Dialogue: The Road to Literacy for Students at Risk in Middle Schools." *Middle School Journal* Vol. 25, No. 4: 50-54.

Goodman, Kenneth S. 1992. "Whole Language Research: Foundations and Development." In *What Research Has to Say About Reading Instruction*. Second edition. Ed. S. Jay Samuels and Alan E. Farstrup, pp. 46-69. Newark, DE: International Reading Association.

Goodman, Y.M., D.J. Watson, and C.L. Burke. 1987. *Reading Miscue Inventory: Alternative Procedures*. Katonah, NY: Richard C. Owen.

Graves, Michael F., Cheryl L. Cooke, and Michael J. Laberge. 1983. "Effects of Previewing Difficult Short Stories on Low Ability Junior High School Students' Comprehension, Recall, and Attitudes." *Reading Research Quarterly* Vol. 18, No. 3: 262-276.

Gross, Patricia A. 1991. "Interactive Reading on the Secondary Level." Paper presented at the Annual Meeting of the National Reading Conference (41st, Palm Springs, CA, December 3-7, 1991). ERIC Document Number 359 490.

Gross, Patricia A. 1992. "Shared Meaning: Whole Language Reader Response at the Secondary Level." Paper presented at the Annual Meeting of the National Reading Conference (42nd, San Antonio, TX, December 2-5, 1992). ERIC Document No. 359 491.

Guzzetti, Barbara J. 1990. "Enhancing Comprehension Through Trade Books in High School English Classes." *Journal of Reading* Vol. 33, No. 6: 411-413.

Hadaway, Nancy L. and Terrell A. Young. 1994. "Content Literacy and Language Learning: Instructional Decisions." *The Reading Teacher* Vol. 47, No. 7: 522-527.

Hafner, Lawrence E., Barbara C. Palmer, and Stan M. Tullos. 1986. "The Differential Reading Interests of Good and Poor Readers in the Ninth Grade." *Reading Improvement* Vol. 23: 39-42.

Haggard, Martha Rapp. 1986. "The Vocabulary Self-Collection Strategy: Using Student Interest and World Knowledge to Enhance Vocabulary Growth." *Journal of Reading* Vol. 29, No. 7: 634-642.

Hayes, David A. and Robert J. Tierney. 1982. "Developing Readers' Knowledge Through Analogy." *Reading Research Quarterly* Vol. 17, No. 2: 256-280.

Helfeldt, John P. and William A. Henk. 1990. "Reciprocal Question-Answer Relationships: An Instructional Technique for At-Risk Readers." *Journal of Reading* Vol. 33, No. 7: 509-514.

Herman, Patricia A., Richard C. Anderson, David P. Pearson, and William E. Nagy. 1987. "Incidental Acquisition of Word Meaning From Expositions With Varied Text Features." *Reading Research Quarterly* Vol. 22, No. 3: 263-284.

Hickey, M. Gail. 1990. "Reading and Social Studies: The Critical Connection." *Social Education* Vol. 33, No. 7: 175-176.

Ianacone, John A. 1993. "Vocabulary Lists: The Ambsace of Word Study." *English Journal* Vol. 82, No. 1: 41-45.

International Reading Association. 1989. "Reading Resource Specialists Make a Difference (Secondary Perspectives)." *Journal of Reading* Vol. 33, No. 2: 138-140.

International Reading Association. 1990. "A Reading-Writing Connection in the Content Areas (Secondary Perspectives)." *Journal of Reading* Vol. 33, No. 5: 376-378.

Jenkins, Joseph R. and Linda M. Jenkins. 1987. "Making Peer Tutoring Work." *Educational Leadership* Vol. 44, No. 6: 64-68.

Johannessen, Larry R. 1994. "Enhancing Response to Literature: A Matter of Changing Old Habits." *English Journal* Vol. 83, No. 7: 66-70.

Johnson, David W. and Roger T. Johnson. 1988. "Critical Thinking Through Structured Controversy." *Educational Leadership* Vol. 45, No. 8: 58-64.

Kellerman, Karen Kennedy. 1991. "Students' Rejection of Teacher Choice of Free Reading Books." M.A. Thesis, Kean College. ERIC Document Number 329 949.

Kletzien, Sharon Benge and Barbara Conway Hushion. 1992. "Reading Workshop: Reading, Writing, Thinking." *Journal of Reading* Vol. 35, No. 6: 444-451.

Knoeller, Christian P. 1994. "Negotiating Interpretations of Text: The Role of Student-Led Discussions in Understanding Literature." *Journal of Reading* Vol. 37, No. 7: 572-80.

Krashen, Stephen. 1993. *The Power of Reading: Insights from the Research*. Englewood, CO: Libraries Unlimited, Inc.

Krogness, Mary Mercer. 1995. *Just Teach Me, Mrs. K: Talking, Reading, and Writing with Resistant Adolescent Learners*. Portsmouth, NH: Heinemann.

Langer, Judith A. 1984. "Examining Background Knowledge and Text Comprehension." *Reading Research Quarterly* Vol. 19, No. 4: 468-481.

Langer, Judith A. 1993. "Approaches Toward Meaning in Low-and High-Rated Readers." Report Series 2.20. Albany, NY: National Research Center on Literature Teaching and Learning. ERIC Document Number 361 650.

Lawrence, Jean M.B. et al. 1993. "Television in the English Curriculum (The Round Table)." *English Journal* Vol. 82, No. 6: 77-79.

Leal, Dorothy June. 1992. "The Nature of Talk about Three Types of Text During Peer Group Discussions." *Journal of Reading Behavior* Vol. 24, No. 4: 313-38.

Leighton, Dolly B. 1991. "Saturating Students With Reading: A Classroom Lab Approach." *English Journal* Vol. 80, No. 6: 81-85.

Lesesne, Teri S. 1991. "Developing Lifetime Readers: Suggestions From Fifty Years of Research." *English Journal* Vol. 80, No. 6: 61-64.

Lutz, Elaine. 1986. "Parent Involvement in the Secondary Reading Program. " *Journal of Reading* Vol. 29, No. 5: 456-458.

MacGregor, Mollie. 1990. "Reading and Writing in Mathematics." In *Language and Mathematics*. Ed. Jennie Bickmore-Brand, pp. 100-108. Portsmouth, NH: Heinemann.

Mallow, Jeffry V. 1991. "Reading Science." *Journal of Reading* Vol. 34, No. 5: 324-338.

Manzo, Anthony V. and Ula Casale Manzo. 1990. "Note Cue: A Comprehension and Participation Training Strategy." *Journal of Reading* Vol. 33, No. 8: 608-611.

Marshall, James D. 1987. "The Effects of Writing on Students' Understanding of Literary Texts." *Research in the Teaching of English* Vol. 21, No. 1: 30-63.

Matthews, Charles E. 1987. "Lap Reading for Teenagers." *Journal of Reading* Vol. 30, No. 5: 410-413.

McWhirter, Anna M. 1990. "Whole Language in the Middle School." *The Reading Teacher* Vol. 43, No. 8: 562-565.

Menke, Deborah and Beth Davey. 1994. "Teachers' Views of Textbooks and Text Reading Instruction: Experience Matters." *Journal of Reading* Vol. 37, No. 6: 464-470.

Miller, Linda J., Frank W. Kohler, Helen Ezell, Kathryn Hoel, and Phillip S. Strain. 1993. "Winning With Peer Tutoring: A Teacher's Guide." *Preventing School Failure* Vol. 37, No. 3: 14-18.

Montague, Marjorie and Michael L. Tanner. 1987. "Reading Strategy Groups for Content Area Instruction." *Journal of Reading* Vol. 30, No. 8: 716-723.

Morrow, Lesley Mandel. 1983. "Home and School Correlates of Early Interest in Literature." *Journal of Educational Research* Vol. 76, No. 4: 221-230.

Morrow, Lesley Mandel, Diane H. Tracey, and Caterina Marcone Maxwell, eds. 1995. *A Survey of Family Literacy in the United States*. Newark, DE: International Reading Association.

Moscrip, Lynn F. 1991. "How to Start a Successful Paperback Book Program." *English Journal* Vol. 80, No. 6: 79-80.

National Center for Education Statistics. 1994a. *NAEP 1992 Trends in Academic Progress*. Washington, DC: U.S. Department of Education.

National Center for Education Statistics. 1994b. *Reading Literacy in the United States. Technical Report*. Washington, DC: U.S. Department of Education.

Neuman, Susan B. 1986. "The Home Environment and Fifth-Grade Students' Leisure Reading." *The Elementary School Journal* Vol. 86, No. 3: 335-343.